from

Zero

to

Sales Hero

HOW TO DOUBLE YOUR SALES AND
INCOME IN LESS THAN IN 90 DAYS

Amy Lemire Simatos, DTM
& Andreas Simatos

AIM Training and Consulting Inc

Chicago   New York   Paris   London   Athens

First AIM Training and Consulting, Inc. softcover edition April 2015
Second AIM Training and Consulting, Inc. softcover edition January 2016

For information or to inquire about bulk discounts, visit AIMwithAmy.com or FromZeroToSalesHero.com

Exterior design by BlackFrogPrinting.com

Interior design by Amy Lemire Simatos and Andreas Simatos

Manufactured in the United States of America

10 9 8 7 6 5 4 3 2 1

ISBN 978-0-9962-2651-6 Printed Edition
ISBN 978-0-9962-2653-0 Kindle Edition

This book is dedicated to all who persevere in spite of obstacles, stay the course during the dark moments, and keep their spirit alive in spite of challenge; for it is those who make a difference in our world and will experience true victory!

CONTENTS

FREE _BONUS CHAPTER_ plus other
FREE BONUS MATERIAL, TOOLS, and TIPS available at
www.FromZeroToSalesHero.com

FOREWARD

By Raymond Aaron, NY Times Best-Seller

It is very rare that I meet someone like Amy who not only has the business sales experience, but also has stood out amongst the crowd as a top sales trainer and coach. What appeals to me the most is that she has also taken a process that can be so complex and has made it so simple, easy to follow and understand. Her unique secrets, best practice sales insights, real life business experience, and commitment to helping others deliver outstanding sales results is unparalleled! After reading this excellent book, I recommend it to others as a must read! I feel this book should be a sales training requirement and mandatory guide for any sales professional, no matter what level — beginner or top performer. Anyone wanting to increase his or her sales, income and business success must read this book! What makes this book so fascinating is that it explains, step by step, what it takes to go from a 'zero' to 'hero' sales performer by following an easy to execute process, best practices, and proven strategy. Amy's secrets from 21 years in sales and top performance are between the covers of this book.

You will take a quantum leap in your business by reading this book; it will dramatically improve your sales closing ability, handling the most difficult objections, and deliver an overall impact on your results you never dreamed possible. If you would like to improve your income, sales success, and quality of life, this book contains the strategy to get you there.

— RAYMOND AARON,
New York Times Bestselling Author and Founder of The Raymond Aaron Group

INTRODUCTION

What inspired me to write a book called 'From Zero to Sales Hero'? I have read so many great books about sales methodology, new ideas, and approaches, but I have not read one about 'what do I do when I am an experienced sales professional and I have hit a sales slump' - or - 'I am newer to sales and I don't know where to start.' This book is for anyone in sales, no matter if you are an experienced professional or someone new to the profession. The principles it takes to be a success in sales are the same regardless of your level.

I spent 21 years in sales. I can say I have sold the full array of products and services, including business-to-business (telecom, payroll/tax service), advancing later in my career to the world of healthcare sales (medical consumables), and in the majority of my career selling medical capital equipment. I can say I am fortunate to have celebrated the moments of glory: standing on the stage at the National Sales Training Meeting, getting my recognition awards, sales plaques, seeing my name in the stack rankings at the top, the congratulatory emails from my director and vice president, making a 6-figure income earning top commissions, and, most importantly, being grateful that what I was selling was going to save someone's life (medication safety software).

But that is not why I wrote this book. I found out how quickly you can go from being a 'sales hero' to a 'sales zero' 3 years ago during one of the most memorable sales years I had ever experienced. How did I turn myself around? I was able to follow the principles outlined in this book to get back to being a 'sales hero.'

About 3 years ago, after I had come off of my best sales year ever, being a top performer, and savoring the victory, my world came crashing down around me. The congratulatory emails I had the previous fiscal year quickly turned to stern warnings about my sales performance the next fiscal year. I sat at 11% of my annual quota midway through the year. Needless to say, I was not only off track with my sales performance, but my attitude, focus, and entire identity of being a 'top sales performer' seemed like a distant memory. I felt like the rug had been pulled out from underneath me. 'What happened?' I asked myself.

I first spent time wallowing in disillusionment; I remember telling myself 'my boss is being too tough on me, the difficult and new customers are taking too much time from last year's success, the timing was bad, the market was down, and on and on.' I was frustrated and humiliated. Then I decided to do something I had always thought about but had never done at rock bottom: I hired a sales coach. That was one of the best decisions I ever made; my coach quickly got me to see that I was making excuses, blaming everything but myself, my poor attitude, lack of activity and focus on failure for where I was. We quickly put together a plan to get me back on track with my sales performance. I began to develop an attitude of accountability vs. victim.

The interesting thing is there is no '1 secret' as to how I was able to go from 11% of my quota to ending the fiscal year at 117%. It was all about 'back to the basics,' which is what I will reveal in this book. 'A salesperson is as successful as what he/she does day in and day out' was a saying I heard at my first outside sales position. That is exactly what I figured out; I had lost touch with what it takes to be successful; I had forgotten how important the principles of sales success were — but once I went back to the basics, my world changed, and so did my sales numbers and performance.

I remember the last day of that sales year. I spent the day with my director, waiting for that last deal to book under $2M. When it came in it was surreal. The congratulatory email from my director to the sales team, along with one from my area vice president, took on a new meaning for me; I had proven I could do it once again. I won't say it was easy; it got tougher before it got easier. Most importantly, I learned from that experience that, if you can pull yourself out of a place you don't want to be, you can do whatever you want. "What the mind can perceive it can achieve" came true to me in my world that day.

This book is dedicated to every sales professional and entrepreneur out there, regardless of where you are with your performance. This is my way of giving back to all who taught me along the journey of going from sales zero to sales hero. I wish you the best of success and hope you find the sales profession not only fun and filled with rewards, but one of the best professional paths you can take to make the difference in the life of someone else.

— AMY LEMIRE SIMATOS, DTM,
Founder, AIM Training and Consulting Inc.

Chapter 1
ATTITUDE IS EVERYTHING

Very often, we are our own worst enemy as we foolishly build stumbling blocks on the path that leads to success and happiness.
— LOUIS BINSTOCK

Focus on success — Do it anyway!

When I first got into B2B (business-to-business) outside sales selling payroll and tax services for businesses, I had a rude awakening. I thought being in outside sales meant living a life of taking clients to lunch, not having to do much if any work, etc. I still remember the first day on the job and my sales manager handing me a thick book of all my accounts and saying, 'OK, start making some calls.'

I had previously come from the world of inside sales, selling cellular/paging services over the phone to inbound callers. The idea of having to look for business through cold calling or prospecting, was a foreign and very scary idea to me. Honestly, the first several weeks on the job, I was disillusioned. I thought I had made a big mistake entering the world of sales asking myself 'is this what it is really all about?'

My mom had been in sales her entire career and I asked her 'Can I really do this, and will I even be a success?' Not only was it about the cold calling, it was about being held accountable making a quota. Plus, I was calling out my weekly appointments, referrals, and calls at a weekly team meeting — not to mention trying to learn a product, although good and valuable to businesses. I came to realize that I had no interest and passion in 'number crunching.'

Six months into it, I wanted to quit. But then one day, a voice of reason came into my head and said: 'Stick with it, learn the basics, build a foundation of what it takes to be successful, and you will one day find another product you are passionate about. But, you must learn the basics of what it takes to be a good salesperson first.' The last 4 letters of the word 'enthusiasm,' represent 'I am sold myself,' when it comes to sales. One year to the day, I left that position and entered the world of selling what I was passionate about: medical products. I had always been interested in health and helping others, so this tied right into my natural interests — I was enthusiastic about it! But my lesson is simple: it was the voice of my positive attitude that got me through that year.

Another way to stay focused on success is to celebrate your wins. After you have done the activity, especially all of the best practices we will review in this book, there is a light at the end of the tunnel. If you follow all of the practices I will share with you, I promise you will see and celebrate the wins.

When I say 'celebrate,' I mean reward yourself such as a gift to yourself, spending time doing a hobby, buying that gadget, or splurging for that favorite outfit you have your eye on. Celebrating and recognizing each win is not only fun, but it reinforces the good behavior and hard work you have done.

Sometimes we think of the win as 'winning the deal,' but a win can be landing an appointment, making your weekly prospecting goal, advancing an opportunity to the next step, bouncing back after a loss or bad sales call, hearing a customer or prospect say 'thank you' because you made their business better by being there with your product or service, or just simply getting the sale, of course. Celebrate all wins.

The power of daily rituals — How to set yourself up for success daily

Daily rituals are critical: One of the things I learned from others and through experience is the importance of developing daily rituals. It's important that you 'fuel' yourself daily, preferably every morning with positive energy, thoughts, and focus. Think of it like fueling your car. Would you put sugar in your gas tank? Of course not!

This also ties into the "Law of Attraction", or the power of manifestation. If you are in a positive state of mind, you will attract great things, including people, money and sales. But if you focus on 'what is wrong,' and how terrible the day is going to be, the fact that you got up on the wrong side of the bed, etc., you will attract disappointment, repel success, and people will not want to be in your presence, and that could mean the key decision maker that will get you the sale you need.

Look, I am not going to say I have never been in a bad state of mind, but what I have come to learn is that my best and most successful days in sales are the ones in which I was in a peak state of mind at the start of the day.

Any sports team or player knows this. You are a performer too! What you focus on manifests — focus and feelings equal results.

(TFAR: Thoughts + Feelings + Actions = Results)

There are many benefits to having a daily ritual. Probably the most important is the fact that it puts you into an awesome state of mind. When I watch teams at a big game getting ready to go on the field, I see them jumping up and down, saying a team chant, and getting really excited about the big game they are getting ready to play. Now I'm not saying that you need to jump up and down and act like you're going to play in a big game like the Super Bowl, but what I am saying is that it's important that you adopt a daily ritual that is going to help get you into the right state of mind for the rest of your day.

It's critical that you schedule this into your daily schedule. It's so easy to not do it and to make excuses such as "I have an early appointment", and then before you know it the day has already started and it is too late. In the next section, I'm going to give you some ideas about how you can do a daily ritual. And if you do have an early morning, there are many ways you can do a ritual that don't take extra time. For example, you can listen to an inspirational or motivational speaker on the way to your appointment. I often used to listen to Tony Robbins, Wayne Dyer, or other speakers who would talk about either sales practices or how to be positive, and they motivated me to get into the right frame of mind before that big appointment.

Ideas for turning daily rituals into habits

What are some ideas for getting into a daily ritual?

- Workout — This also helps release the 'feel good' endorphins!
- Meditate
- Read self-empowering books and articles
- Say daily affirmations — I used to do this when I would work out: 'Every day and every way, miracles, money, and opportunity come my way!'
- Pray to your spiritual leader
- Listen to music
- Listen to motivational speakers — I often did this in my car on the way to my sales appointments
- Yoga
- Keep a daily gratitude journal — I do this daily by listing '10 things I am grateful for today'
- Listen to a podcast
- Stretch
- Take a walk

- Talk to a coach or accountability partner
- Sing
- Dance
-
- Cherish your spouse or children
- Cherish your pet
- Deep breathing
- Experience nature

Activity = Results

Early in my sales career when I was selling payroll and tax services to emerging businesses, I received some of the best training that helped me learn the basic principles of what it takes to be successful in sales. In their nationally recognized sales training programs, one of the biggest focuses of their program that I learned was the importance of activity – hourly, daily, and weekly – to hit your monthly sales target.

Anytime my performance slipped, I could see a direct correlation between activity and results. I remember the Monday morning meeting when we would call out our numbers from the previous week, specifically how many prospect calls, appointments, referrals from banks/CPAs, and sales we obtained. Then we had set times when we had to be in the office for 'phone canvassing,' also know as prospecting. Like many of my counterparts, I was never fond of this, especially if our boss was in the office listening in over our cubicle walls. But looking back, it all made sense — it was all about driving momentum in our sales funnel, and also developing new habits and doing consistent activity.

Prospecting is a numbers game. I must give my mom credit here. She has also spent her career in sales and sales training. When I was new in sales, she told me that 'Prospecting is like a bag of M&M's. You have to go through the bag and see the green, red, brown, and all colors. The green ones are the ones that will end up buying from us.' In other words, there is no sense in getting upset when someone says 'no' to you. Say 'thank you' and move to the next prospect!

Later in my career when my sales numbers hit an all-time low, I hired a coach; after he listened to my sob story about how terrible my life and sales results were, he asked me to record and send him a copy of where and how I spent every hour of my past work week. At first I thought 'oh, that's easy,' then came the time to do the task. Wow! It was a wakeup call.

I came to realize that much of my activity and time was unaccounted for, or was spent on wasteful activities, projects, conference calls, and other time-sucking activities that were not only distractions, but were in no way going to get me to hit my number. No wonder I was not where I needed to be with my numbers! I re-committed to doing my weekly prospect calls. In addition, I set up a weekly 'Activity Accountability' tracker to track my weekly call, appointment, and sales targets. I made it a weekly habit again. I went from being an underperformer at 11% of plan to a top sales performer at 117% of my quota as a result. (See my BONUS SECTION at www.FromZeroToSalesHero.com for an activity tracker you can use).

Miracles happen when you do the activity

The idea of prospecting, not just on the phone but also in person, will pay off. I remember one particular Friday afternoon when I was in business-to-business sales, I had set the time in my calendar to get out to my territory and visit some of the local businesses, or 'foot canvassing' as we called it. I remember pulling up in front of an older, industrial looking building and, being newer in sales and fearing the rejection, my self-talk was 'Why am I here? They probably don't need any tax or payroll help.' As I walked in and introduced myself, I said my 'Hello, can I talk to the person in your office who manages taxes and payroll?' The receptionist looked at me, smiled, and said, 'Yes.' As I waited, up walked the Office Manager. I introduced myself and told her I was with a payroll and tax service company. She replied, 'I am so glad you are here! The accounting company we work with for our payroll has not returned our calls and we need to run payroll checks in 2 days. Can you help us?' She seemed frantic as she told her story. 'Of course I can!' I replied. She signed all the paperwork on the spot, gave me an order, and gave me her payroll information.

Yes, I got an order on a Friday afternoon at 4 pm just because I was out doing my prospecting! You never know what can happen when you do the activity. And ever since that win, I made a habit throughout my sales career to do some of my weekly prospecting on Friday afternoons; most people are in a good mood before the weekend, and they may be more open to talking to you.

I often coach sales team members who are struggling with making their numbers. One common theme is when I ask them 'How much time are you prospecting each week?' The typical response is 'I am too busy,' or they review their schedule to try to convince me 'they have no time' to do this. I never buy that. Think about it — if you were a top performer on a sports team, would you neglect practicing? Of course not!

What is the recipe to success? First of all, work smarter, not harder. Lack of prospecting often leads to stress and scrambling at the end of the month, quarter, or even worse, the fiscal year to make your number. This is not a fun place to be. For those of you new in sales, the more you prospect, the better you get, the more contacts you make, the more money you make — and you can also have fun while doing it!

Another common mistake is to have a sales funnel of opportunities focused only on a couple 'elephant, or big deals' to hit quota. The sales funnel should have a quantity of quality opportunities of many sizes. Work harder not smarter. Plan your work, work your plan — plan your week.

You become whom you associate with

What else can you do to keep your attitude at its best? Avoid toxic people, whiners, bad/unhealthy habits (smoking, etc.), and getting caught up in the water cooler talk. Hey, I am not going to say that I never ever called my peers to vent, because I do believe we all need to download when we have had a bad sales call, lost a sale, had the rug pulled out from under us, etc., in order to let it go. But choose when and who you do this with carefully; maybe someone outside your work. I would have one friend on my sales team that I would vent to. But, we would also encourage each other and celebrate our successes as well as brainstorm ideas and strategies about getting new connections, overcoming objections, and making sales.

Calling everyone on your sales team and complaining about how bad things are leads to bad consequences. It can get back to your boss or give you a reputation as a 'Pigpen' (I think of the Charlie Brown character that always had an 'aura' of smell and dirt around him). It can also give you a reputation of 'energy suck'. I think we can all understand that 'energy suck' is the person who no one wants to be around, and when they are, the energy is sucked out of the room. The last reason is this can come back to haunt you later; I have witnessed it on several occasions. After having spent over 21 years in corporate America, I have been through several mergers, acquisitions, and reorganizations, many of which ended in a reduction of force. I remember most of the team members that didn't survive these cuts were the ones who did more of complaining than contributing to the overall good of the team.

It wasn't always about making the numbers. You can also be taken out of consideration for future promotions. Recently, I was talking to someone on a sales team who was going for a promotion to a Key Account Manager. The person told me they were upset over the compensation plan, the territory, team changes, etc. Ironically, I found out a week later that he didn't get the promotion — the #1 reason being his attitude. One of my favorite sayings is 'think of the shadow you cast.'

The moral of the story is to surround yourself with positive people and those whom you wish to become. Talk to others who are successful on your sales team and outside your sales team, and, most importantly, get a mentor.

When I was new in my sales position, I looked at the rankings to see who was doing the best and I reached out to them and asked 'Hey, you seem to be doing well. Can I pick your brain?' To this day, I never heard 'no', and, as a matter of fact, most people were more than happy to talk to me and flattered that I reached out to them. Find a mentor, and as you grow, be a mentor. If you lose a sale or don't land the appointment you want, do not beat yourself up. Instead, ask 'How can I learn from this?' The worst thing to do is wallow in it — it will have a ripple effect in a bad way on future success.

Chapter 2
THE SECRET SAUCE: ACCOUNTABILITY

One important key to success is self-confidence. An important key to self-confidence is preparation.
— ARTHUR ASHE

Results or reasons?

Invest in the power of goal setting. It will give you the focus you need to be a success. There are many books you can use to set your goals. One of my favorites is 'Goals,' by Brian Tracy. Every New Year, I write out my goals and I break them down by month. I don't call them 'resolutions!' Why? People are notorious for not keeping resolutions! In my experience, putting a goal in writing is putting it out to the universe that you are serious about it. As I look back at the end of the year, I see that I have achieved the majority of the goals I write.

One of the practices that I do weekly is to sit down every Sunday night and write out my goals for the week. Each month, I write out what my targets would be for the month so that I can ensure I am going to hit them. This is all driven by the number I need to hit for my annual quota. Never aim for 100%; aim higher! Because if you miss, you will still be at 100%.

One of the biggest risks we run by not setting our goals is that we end the month without the results we need to keep us on track for the yearly quota. Then, we feel like we are under pressure and stress. We feel under pressure from our manager. We run the risk of pressuring our customers to buy from us when they are not ready. We even may look 'desperate' to make a sale. I have seen this happen all too often in the sales profession. We push the customer so hard that they end up not only pushing back on us and saying no, but they ask us not to call or come back again.

Unfortunately, I think this is part of the reason the sales profession and sales people get a bad reputation! I have had years where I made my quota mid-year, and I have had years where I was down to the wire making my annual number at the end of the year. There is no feeling like making your annual number months or quarters before the sales year is over! The pressure is off! (It's even better each time I exceeded 100% of my quota, providing me with incredible over-achievement payouts.)

If you are not hitting your numbers or sales: How are you spending your time? Try the 1/3 rule. 1/3 of your time should be prospecting and qualifying new business opportunities. 1/3 of time shoule be to manage your current opportunities in your pipeline.

And, 1/3 of your time should be creating customers for life (e.g. – quarterly business reviews, additional business, referrals, new product offerings). Block time for prospecting. Once again, the more contacts you make, the more money you make. Prospecting is the lifeblood success in sales. Without prospecting, you cannot develop the new sales opportunities that will develop into sales — and your income.

In my experience, the step that often gets neglected the most is the qualifying and prospecting step. Often we spend more time managing our current opportunities and hoping that the big elephant deal is going to come this month, or for the quarter, or for the year. When we look at our pipeline of opportunities, it's important that the opportunities are qualified, determining when opportunities are legitimate while also trying not to be over-confident. They should also have velocity, meaning that they are moving through the sales pipeline at a good pace. Finally, the pipeline should have a good quantity of opportunities to make your number for the year. As a matter of fact, a good idea is to have three to five times the opportunities in your pipeline as your annual quota. That way, if you have a deal that slips or is lost, you still have enough opportunities to make your quota.

The rewards of *just doing it*

When you do your activity, even when you don't want to, there are many rewards. Improved self-confidence, overcoming your fear of cold calling, making sales numbers, getting the recognition for your performance, and making a high sales achiever income are just a few examples of the rewards of doing the activity it takes to be successful in sales. Sometimes I check in with sales representatives who are not hitting their sales numbers. When I talk to them, one of the things they often tell me is that they don't make prospecting calls. They say that they are 'too busy, have to travel to appointments, don't have time, et cetera et cetera.'

I find myself having to remind them that if you are not making prospect calls, your business is at risk in your territory. Plus, it is going to be very difficult to make your number if you are not putting new opportunities into your pipeline, which is driven by the prospecting activity. What I often remind them is that this is a number one priority and should be scheduled in their calendar. I used to have a weekly spreadsheet in which I set up my weekly call, appointment, sale, and referral tracking.
I remember there were some weeks when it would be a Friday afternoon, and I would realize that I had not made all of my calls for the week. There I would

be, late on a Friday afternoon, getting the work done. I remember I would always feel proud of myself that I got the work done even when I did not want to, and honestly it really became fun after a while to make the calls and the connections that I needed to do to make my numbers.

Another area where we seem to fall short in activity is doing the right discovery and needs analysis in the account. It's very easy to walk into an account and start telling people about the product or service we are offering without qualifying the opportunity first. The risk that we have is that it makes it very difficult to ask for a commitment if we have not uncovered any problems or needs from the customer or earned the right to ask for the sale with the key decision-maker.

The other challenge is that it makes us look like the competitor who just came in the door if we are not finding the needs that can uniquely differentiate us from our competition. Doing discovery is critical and vital to the sales process, which we will talk about in a later chapter.

Last, some are afraid of the 'closing' or asking for commitment. We will review all of the steps of the sales process in detail later in this book. If you have qualified the opportunity and done the right discovery to understand what the prospect's needs are and if you have positioned your solution as the way to help them get from their current state to their desired state, closing should be simple. By closing, you are asking them to agree that you can help them resolve their business needs while re-stating the issues they told you they are facing.

If you think about it, we are all experts at taking action in one or more areas of life. For example, we may be great at getting to the gym or spending time with family and friends. But, we may not be great at doing what it takes to be successful in sales. In this scenario, we need to take a look at where we are doing well and ask ourselves "What is it that I'm doing in this area of my life that makes me get the results I want?" Then, we need to take a look at the area of our life where we're not getting the results we want and ask ourselves where our focus is. Often when we are falling short, we are focused on fear or failure — instead of success.

How to build the skill of accountability

If you are struggling with keeping yourself accountable, here are some other ideas:

- Set weekly targets — Calls, Appointments, Sales, Wins. See the BONUS SECTION for the accountability Tracker at: www.FromZeroToSalesHero.com
- Get a coach or accountability buddy.
- Ask the experts: Talk to others who are making their sales targets — how are they doing it?
- Hold yourself to a higher standard.
- Think of your sales territory as your personal business franchise. If you have your own business, think of accountability as the lifeblood of your sales-revenue coming in.
- Say NO when you need to and if you are not sure ask: is this activity going to help me advance my sales opportunities and results?
- Reward yourself for doing the work.
- Send your activity tracker to a coach or accountability partner every week.
- Put positive affirmations on your laptop screen – e.g. sticky notes that say positive statements such as "If it's to be it's up to me!"
- If you are prospecting or making customer calls at your desk, put a small mirror there so you can watch yourself smiling as you make the calls. 'Keep smiling and start dialing' I used to say to myself!
- Celebrate any time that you get an appointment, make a sale or advance a sales opportunity; jump

up and down and shout 'YES!' and you will feel great!

Holding you — and your prospect — accountable

In addition to holding ourselves accountable for our activity and our commitments to our numbers, there are going to be times when we also have to hold our prospects and customers accountable for their commitments they make to us. This is sometimes easier said than done in my experience, especially when the stakes are high, tensions are up, and your sales number is on the line.

One year, I was one deal from making my number for the year. The pressure was on because we were in the beginning of the last month of the fiscal year. To say I was feeling the stress was an understatement. The other issue was that I had one key contact in the account who was my sponsor, and she needed to push the envelope in her organization to make the contract get signed.

We had a large order discount on the table for a sign-off by June 30, our fiscal year end. I had asked her several times. I was beginning to get nervous and uncomfortable with asking her for another update and if she had made an advance with the other key decision makers as she had promised to in order to get approval on our contract and order. Then my phone rang. One of my counterparts just brought in her big deal for the end of the year. At first I was frustrated thinking 'Why can't that be me?' Then, I became more motivated and realized that if it's to be, it's up to me.

I picked up my phone and asked my prospect in one of my ways that anyone is receptive to 'I have a favor to ask of you,' to take the internal steps she had agreed to be accountable for. She finally did what she needed to. That advanced my sales opportunity, and we closed it for year-end. In addition to holding yourself accountable, hold your prospects accountable for the commitments they make to you, especially if you have made a concession to them in a negotiation.

Avoid the 'blame game'

Let's face it. When we are not getting the results that we want, the easiest thing to do is to blame everything outside of ourselves. I think we can all relate to that. I will admit I have been guilty of this myself, but over the years I tried to get better at catching myself. I also tried to avoid people that could be toxic and always continue to blame everything around themselves for their poor performance and attitude.

In my Sales Trainer role, I get to interact with both new and tenured sales team members. I often check in with both groups and ask 'How are things going?' If they are stuck or not making the sales numbers, one of the first things I hear on our introductory call is how bad they have it. Excuses include the boss is being difficult, something happened in the territory last year, the competitor pulled the rug out from underneath them, the deal that was lost, the rep before me left the territory a mess, the market is bad, our product has issues, etc.

The next question I ask is: How are you personally accountable for where your results are today? There is usually a pause, then a realization that they are where they are by not being accountable for their personal results. I have always found that blame is the 'easy way out,' and it's much easier to point fingers at the past or others rather than to look in the mirror and see we are at cause for where we are with our results.

Don't get in the habit of the blame game. It will not get you to where you want to be or to your sales numbers for that matter. Instead, make a habit of looking at yourself in the mirror, and asking 'what can I do differently right now to turn this situation around? How am I responsible for this situation and the results that I have at this moment?'

If you have made a mistake, learn from it — especially if you have lost a sale. The best thing you can do is ask yourself 'What have I learned from this and what would I do differently next time?' I also often see sales representatives lose a sale and go into a self-sabotage mode. Other questions to ask if you lose a sale: Did I skip any steps of the sales process (e.g. – discovery, finding a why, etc.)? Did I see any red flags in the opportunity that I chose to ignore? Was I overconfident in this opportunity and did I over-forecast?

Setting a higher standard

What does setting a higher standard mean? To me it means many things. First of all, it means that if we want to be a leader, we need to expect more from ourselves than others do. It is about consistently raising the bar for the results we want. It is about committing to being a top performer, a sales hero, not an average performer! It is about keeping our commitments by being honest and having integrity in all of our interactions with both our internal and external customers. It is about treating others with respect regardless of what level they are in your organization or a customer's organization. Don't judge others even when they are not responding in the way that you want. I have learned many times that you never know how much power somebody has to influence your opportunity, regardless of what their title is. And everybody knows somebody!

I learned the lesson to not judge or react to others during a presentation. I remember one time I was on an appointment doing a demonstration and brief presentation of my product. I was presenting to about three staff nurses and a nursing manager inside the chief nursing officer's office. The chief nursing officer was in the background half-watching my presentation. At one point, he went over to his keyboard and started typing on his computer. I remember at first I felt offended and thought it was rude that he was typing and not paying attention while I was doing my demonstration.

But, I stayed focused. I kept a smile on my face and I kept going. At the end of the demonstration, I asked the nurses what they liked about the product. He quickly chimed in and said to me 'While you were standing and doing your demonstration and presentation, I was typing an e-mail to the chief logistics officer telling them that we absolutely need to move forward with your product.' I learned two lessons from the situation. First, I did not think the chief nursing officer had much influence in this particular account so I'm glad I kept my standards high. Second, it taught me to remain focused on the task at hand no matter what distraction was going on with the audience and not to take it personally.

If you are ever have a question about something you are about to do in a sales opportunity, one question you can ask yourself is 'Would I be okay if this was on the front page of the newspaper?' When I became a sales field trainer, a role that I took on while I was a sales representative, I quickly came to realize that all eyes were on me. Everything I talked about with the new hires was going to be taken very literally. I realized at that moment it was up to me to set a higher standard so that the new hire could aspire to that. One of the top qualities I look for in a sales field trainer, when working with and mentoring a sales new hire, is they must be the 'shadow of a leader.'

The power of saying NO — We do more for others than we will do for ourselves

Life balance is critical to keeping yourself accountable in your sales and business life. You must 'keep your house in order.' Maintain balance between work, family, and your personal life. It seems like when we are doing great in one area of our life, sometimes another area is suffering. During the times my sales results were not where I wanted them to be, I was typically 'overcommitted' to volunteer activities outside work.

A good example is when I was excelling in Toastmasters. It was the year I got my Distinguished Toastmaster Award (an award received by about 5% of Toastmasters worldwide) in 2012, which took me 4 years to achieve, by giving speeches and serving in certain officer roles. That year it also meant I had to serve in a volunteer leadership role as an Area Governor in Chicago — I felt like I got my Masters in Public Speaking, and it was worth it! I was also involved in my church vestry (board of directors) that year, which ended up being more of a time commitment than I initially anticipated. Plus, there were political issues that I didn't realize would become a distraction.

From all of these extracurricular activities, the good news is that I became a better speaker and leader, but my career and the time I was spending at home with my family were taking a negative hit. This often left me feeling overwhelmed, even at points when I felt distracted during the day when thinking about the next meeting I had to go to that night. I learned over the years to get better at saying 'no' and laying down more personal boundaries, and I know that I had to go through this experience to learn that.

'When you say No, what are you saying Yes to?' I also schedule my week every Sunday to avoid last-minute commitments that will take my time. I started to eliminate activities from my life that were not bringing me value or getting me to where I wanted to be long-term. It was difficult, but overall, I feel much more at peace.

Chapter 3
THE ROADMAP TO SUCCESS:
THE SALES PROCESS

If we all did the things we are capable of doing, we would literally astound ourselves.
— THOMAS A EDISON

Every profession has a recipe for success

Every profession has a recipe for success that guarantees the result we pay for as consumers. For example, would you ever get on a plane if a pilot told you that he was not going to follow the flight plan, or skip the pre-flight checklist? Would an NFL football team ever go into the Super Bowl without a playbook? Of course not! But, all too often we forget that there is a specific sales process that we need to follow with any sales opportunity, no matter how large or small it is.

You may be asking: Why is there a sales process? I ask this question in my sales trainings and everyone agrees that the process is to help drive results, improve predictability and forecasting accuracy, and help everyone at every level of the sales organization speak the same language — everyone from the operations team, customer service, field sales, sales leadership, sales training, and all the way up to sales executive leadership. It gives you a competitive edge. For a business to succeed, whether you are working for a company or own your own business, this is critical. Because it helps keep a business in business by predicting incoming sales and revenue and helping resources coordinate upcoming internal processes for new accounts by which it ensures there is enough product on hand to meet the new sales contracts for product and service delivery.

I think each one of the industries I spent time in sales had a 'sales process,' — telecom, tax/payroll service, and medical sales. They are all very similar. I have had a 5-step close process, 7-step sales process, and other variations. Even though the number of steps and the names of the individual steps vary, one thing is consistent: if you want to be a success in sales, there is a distinct, step-by-step process you must follow.

As I look back on my sales career, there were times I followed the process that made sales of which I am going to talk about in this chapter. Also when I looked at the top sales performers and the mentors that I had, they were following their sales processes consistently. Yes, I will confess, there were times I wanted to 'do it my way' and skip steps. I justified it by saying 'Well, this opportunity is different that the other ones, and it's okay if I skip a step.' But, it was very rare that the deals ever closed. They usually pushed out month-to-month, or were lost to a competitor. A valuable and painful lesson to learn that 'doing it my way' is not a good idea when it comes to the sales process.

The risk of 'doing it my way' and skipping the sales process

As I look back on my career, as I mentioned, I confess there are times that I would try to 'do it my way' or gain a false sense of confidence. I thought that I could still get the sale by skipping steps of the process, primarily by either going directly to presenting my product or going to ask for a commitment before I had really done all the proper discovery to ask what the real customer needs were. I sometime did not earn the right to know whether or not my product would really be a fit. The other reason I would skip a step was that I would think, 'I will save time and I have got to get this deal in this month!' Bad decision.

Looking back on my sales career and also with sales representatives that I coach, the majority of the time deals were lost or delayed past the projected close date were not because the competitor had a better product or price. Rather, it was because the steps of the sales process had not been followed. In my experience, not following the sales process often led to those tough discussions that we all dread; with having to explain why our deal was lost to our sales manager!

In my sales training role, sometimes I would listen in to sales leadership calls or attend regional meetings, in which the sales team or sales leadership would be reporting on the opportunities they were working on. The good news is that most of the time it was clear that the sales representatives or leaders had done the right discovery and found reasons or the 'why' for the customer to buy our solution.

However, there were also many situations where it was clear that the sales team member had a lot more work to do uncover the reasons the customer should buy, and why our solution was best vs. the competition to resolve the customer need. Their reasons that the customer was going to buy were based on product features or benefits vs. needs. The problem is they were forecasting the close of an opportunity for either that month or that quarter, and it was very clear that they really did not understand specifically how we could help the customer with our solution. Or, the customer 'why' was weak, meaning the sales rep had not really 'earned the right' to ask the customer to commit to the business.

What are the basic steps of the sales process?

I have combined my 21 years of selling with my many different methodologies the following basic steps as a starting point:

- Prospecting – Qualify the Ideal Prospect
- Discovery - Finding a Why
- Find a Sponsor
- Teach Insights
- Present Your Solution
- Negotiate
- Close – Ask for the Commitment
- Create a Customer for Life

Let's go into more specific detail about each step:

Prospecting – Qualify the ideal prospect: I firmly believe two things when it comes to building your sales funnel and pipeline. First, you must prospect to fill your sales funnel. Second, you must carefully qualify your prospects. Think of the '80/20 rule': 80% of your business will come from 20% of your prospects or accounts on your list.

For example, when I was in medical sales, I had over 250 accounts on my account list that I could call on. There is no way that I would have been able to spend all of my time working with this many prospects. Therefore, I created a TIP Sheet (a Template of my Ideal Prospect. (See www.FromZeroToSalesHero.com for this free BONUS template). It is important that you get all criteria of what your ideal prospect is.

For example, they may need to have a certain number of employees, revenue, or other industry-specific standards that are important to you. This also keeps you from wasting valuable time on accounts or prospects that will never be qualified to buy from you in the end.

Discovery – Finding a *why*: Doing the discovery step is all about finding the needs of the prospect or account to develop this into a future opportunity. We are meeting with key stakeholders and finding out what types of problems they have and whether or not we can help them resolve those problems. We are also beginning to build a business case that we will later present to the customer

The most important reason that we must do discovery is that we must find a *why*. A *why* is what will compel the customer to buy. It is also something that has urgency and needs to be addressed. It means there is something that you find that will cost the customer money or something else if they don't fix the issue. In other words, it must be measurable. We are helping the customer to see their 'current state,' and the 'desired state,' so that we can help them build a vision and a roadmap to get them to the desired state.

Finding a sponsor: At this point, you have done your discovery, and found a *why* that is measurable, is an urgent need, and a significant reason the customer should buy. The next key step is to find the right sponsor. In my sales experience, the majority of the time I was working with multiple contacts. I always found there was at least one key sponsor who held the ultimate power and authority to execute the final decision and make the sale final. This is also the person that can say yes when everyone else is saying no to your solution, and they have signature authority to sign off on your order.

All too often, we confuse a coach or a friend in our opportunity as the sponsor. We find out at the end of the sales cycle that this person does not have the wherewithal, political power, or ammunition internally to execute our order within the organization. We have wasted our time, and our opportunity is now delayed.

Teach insights: The prospect and customer of today is much different than the prospect or customer of the past. Today, our prospects are interested in hearing our insights. For example, what do we know about our industry or recent trends that could help them make the right decision? What are some of the blind spots they are not seeing about the way they are making their decision? Are they making price the top priority over value? How can you be a trusted advisor to the hospital and bring them valuable information that will help them to make the right decision?

I'm informing the customer of things that they may not want to hear. Prospects buy your insights, not your products, in the sales process. But at the end of the day, you are serving them and building your personal credibility by helping them avoid making a costly mistake.

Present your solution: After you have done the right discovery as well as found the right sponsor and taught them some unique industry insights, you are ready to present your solution. Some of the basics about presenting your solutions include always presenting your proposal in person. When you send somebody a proposal via e-mail, there are two risks. First, they may not read your e-mail. Second, they may get pricing information to compare you to your competitor.

If you must send your proposal via e-mail, make sure that you can set up a phone call, or better yet, a WebEx with videoconferencing so that you can watch your prospect as they review your proposal.

Negotiate: Since this is such an important step in the sales process, I have dedicated an entire future chapter to the subject. The bottom line is that negotiating can become a very emotional activity for both the seller and the prospect. Personal stakes can run high. You may be asked to make concessions, and it's very easy to give away your power during the negotiation if you're not careful.

I truly believe that 'whoever speaks last loses when it comes to negotiations.' What that really means is that we must be comfortable with silence, healthy tension, and saying no to unreasonable requests during negotiations. If we are not comfortable with silence and healthy tension during the negotiation, we may say too much, and it diminishes our personal power. When you ask a question, wait seven seconds for the response.

Close – Ask for the commitment: For many sales reps I talk to, this seems to be the most difficult step of the entire sales process. My thoughts are that if you have done the sales process the right way by accomplishing all of the previous steps, you have earned the right to ask for the business. But if we have not earned the right at the end of the sales process, I think we know that the customer may push back on our asking for the commitment. We are uncomfortable asking for the commitment and fear a negative response.

One way I close my opportunities is to summarize to the customer the three ways that my solution is positioned to help resolve their business issues, and then ask them if they agree that it makes sense to move forward with a solution.

Create a customer for life: After the sale has been closed for you, creating a customer for life is critical to your future business. First, happy customers can be a source of referrals. Second, they can also be a source of additional or future business. Third, it's also important that you have some good reference site accounts for your future prospect accounts.

One way to keep a customer for life is to under-promise and over-deliver. Also schedule quarterly business reviews (QBR) to review the current state of their business with you. (See the free BONUS section in www.zerotosaleshero.com for a sample

Customer QBR template). You can review current business, any issues they are facing so that you can help resolve these, as well as giving the customer a view of what your company has for future opportunities for them, and products or services. There is nothing worse than inheriting an account where your customer says 'I haven't seen a rep from your company in ages!' Don't be that person!

What is the *Why*? No problem, No deal!

The biggest mistake in the sales process is asking for a commitment before the customer sees that you have brought them a clear way to resolve their 'current state' business issues. An unqualified, unmotivated buyer will not buy. People buy for emotional reasons, and they justify with logic. In other words, an undisturbed buyer will not see any value in changing if they don't have a critical reason to change.

Here is an example: When the new iPhone version came out, a friend, an IT expert, was excited, and told me 'You need to get one of these.' He went on to tell me about all the features, new enhancements, improved camera, etc. I said 'The iPhone that I have now is fine; I really don't need to spend the several hundred dollars to change phones right now.' In other words, I had no *why* or reason to change. Then, a week later, as I was getting out of my car in my garage, my iPhone somehow slipped from my grip and landed on the concrete floor. I looked and my heart sank — the screen was cracked and there were a variety of colors and lines across it. I first thought, 'I can still use it', then I realized even the home button was not working nor was the touchscreen. I lost the ability to email or use it as a phone.

My mind started racing. It was the end of the sales month and quarter. I needed my iPhone to check my email and was on standby for a large sale and purchase order that would help me hit my number. My boss was also counting on it and had scheduled a phone call in 30 minutes to provide him with an update. Plus, the customer had already called me several times that day asking for negotiations and special delivery conditions of which I was unsure I could meet. Lastly, I had a meeting that evening, and I had planned to use the navigation app to find the meeting.

Reality began to set in. Without my iPhone, I was frozen in my tracks. I quickly called my IT friend from my landline phone and told him what happened. I said how now the iPhone was now a must for me. That is what having a *why* is all about — a compelling reason why the prospect cannot live without what you have to sell them!

Behind every sale is a sponsor

Before you can get a final commitment, there needs to be a sponsor for your opportunity. This is especially important if you are in a complex sale with multiple contacts in the account. At the end of the day, there is usually only one person who has the political power, authority, and ability to say yes when everyone else says no, as well as signing off on your order. In other words, this is the person who also has the VETO power. Some good questions and points to consider during the sales process are:

- Who is the ultimate decision maker, or sponsor?
- Am I influencing the key decision maker?
- Who will sign off on your order?
- Is there anyone else that will make the influence on this decision (e.g. – a board of directors or committee)?
- If I can't get access to the sponsor early in the sales process, who can I connect with that can influence the sponsor? The sooner you identify that person, the better.
- Get to the point with the sponsor: What's in it for me (WIIFM)?

In my experience, getting to the sponsor in a complex sale is not always an easy task. There are administrative assistants, gatekeepers, and/or a myriad of other people, projects, and internal issues all demanding time from your sponsor. But here is an idea: Get out! This means get outside the account's 4 walls. Sponsors are everywhere, including trade shows, chapter meetings, local forums, etc.

I used to go to the quarterly Nursing Leadership Meeting Chapter in my home state. I was the only vendor that was ever invited to these meetings. I was invited after I hosted an 'educational evening' about how I was helping hospitals improve quality and safety outcomes in the state. Also, I signed up for local chapter of IT, Biomed, and Healthcare Executives. I would then attend their chapter meetings, forums, and conferences. Not only did I make some great contacts that were later sponsors in my sales opportunities, but also I couldn't help but notice that none of my competitors were ever there.

I also had another prospect that invited me to a chapter meeting where there were no other vendors present but myself. This is another great place I made contacts and future sponsors. I also received more industry insights by listening to speakers talk about top of mind challenges and issues in the healthcare industry. The lesson here is that it is much easier to connect with sponsors outside of their day-to-day appointment schedule. They are not on a 'time limit' and usually appreciate the fact you have taken time to attend their event. They see you have taken an interest in their business. Better yet, if you have the option to donate or sponsor the event, you have definitely earned the right to be there!

The top mistakes sellers make that you can avoid in finding the serious buyer

- Spending too much time in your sales opportunities with someone who cannot and lacks the power to make the decision, a 'friend' or a 'talker.'
- 'Feel good' appointments — meeting people to have meetings on your calendar, or to feel 'busy' and conducting a meeting without a strategy or plan.
- Being 'afraid' to call on the top sponsor or decision maker. Remember, they put their pants on one leg at a time like we all do!
- Not bringing value to your meeting with the sponsor (e.g., industry insights).

- Not getting to know the sponsor outside the hospital (e.g., trade groups, chapter meetings, etc.).
- Not being prepared or on time for your meeting. I used to create a brief agenda for important meetings to stay on task.
- Not having multiple sponsors. In complex sales with multiple decision makers, you will need multiple sponsors. Don't put all your 'eggs in 1 basket.' What if your sponsor leaves during your sales process? I have seen this happen. For example, having a separate clinical, financial, and operational sponsor was critical in my healthcare sales process.
- Not knowing your sponsor before the meeting For example, use Linked In, web sites, and other sources to learn what awards have they won and what are they known for.
- Not following up with the sponsor within 24 hours of your meeting with a 'thank you' and any additional information or action you committed to take on their behalf.
- Lack of pre-call planning — not knowing what you are going to talk about before the call or not writing your discovery questions in advance.
- Forgetting to decide what 'advance' or outcome you want as a result of the call, such as a next meeting that includes additional key stakeholders for example.

Chapter 4
WHAT IT TAKES TO BE A SALES HERO: BE A TRUSTED ADVISOR

It is in the moments of decision that your destiny is shaped.
— ANTHONY ROBBINS

The biggest mistakes to avoid in selling

In all my years of selling, there are some clear ways that will guarantee that you will lose your credibility, the opportunity for a second meeting, and even worse, the sale or the opportunity altogether. Here is a top 10 list of what to avoid:

- **Being dishonest**...About your product features, future promises, capabilities that do not exist, and the list goes on.
- **Putting down your competition**...In front of a customer or prospect. This gives the impression you are desperate and not trustworthy.
- **Being late** — I love the phrase 'Lombardi time'; make it a habit to arrive 15 minutes early no matter what. And if there is some reason you can't be there on time, let your appointment know.
- **Over-promising and under-delivering** — Instead, try under-promising and over-delivering

everything to your customer and also in terms of your sales forecasting. Don't get into a situation where you are over-promising at the end of the sales month and then come up short. It only damages your credibility.

- **Forgetting an important document for your meeting** — "The devil is in the details," and I know it has happened to all of us. We are ready to leave for that big meeting, and we realize we forgot to print that proposal. The printer jams, and we are flustered. Get into a habit of getting all of these items printed and ready for the meeting the day or night before. That includes being sure there is gas in your car! You don't want to have to stop for gas or run out of gas on the way to an important appointment.

- **Outnumbering the customer** — This means if you are meeting with one person, the most you should bring with you is one person. Yes, there may be extenuating circumstances, such as if you are giving a presentation with multiple presenters. But, it really creates an awkward energy and environment for the customer or prospect when they are sitting across from 3 suits. If you need to decide who should really be at the meeting, ask your team members what value they will bring to the meeting. Let the prospect/customer know who is coming with you to the meeting in advance.

- **Not knowing the competition inside and out** — Know who your competitors are and why you are better. You need to know not only who your competitors are. But, you also need to know what they offer and what makes your product or service unique and a better offering. What landmines is the competitor planting for you?

- **Pressuring a customer to buy because you are under pressure** — I confess that I have been here before. But, the issue at hand is that when we are under pressure to make our number for the month, quarter, or year, we show up in front of the customer in a different way. We stop listening, and we begin to turn off the customer, possibly to the point where they don't want to do business with us at all. Be careful. One of my mentor sales directors always told me 'If what you are about to do could damage a personal relationship, don't do it.'

- **Talking more than the customer or prospect** — Yes, there are times when this is okay, such as when you are doing a product demo or giving a presentation. But you should still ask check-in questions in these situations, such as 'Does this make sense?' The more the customer or prospect talks, the more you learn, the more they feel in control, and the more they sell themselves on you and your product.

- **Too much contact** – Research and evidence has shown that the best sales performers have fewer touch points with the prospect. They have a plan for every meeting, and they advance their sales opportunity at each customer-facing meeting. When you have a meeting, ensure there is a succinct purpose and you are not 'having a meeting to have a meeting,' aka the 'feel good appointment.' Not only are you wasting the customer's time, you are wasting yours, and they may not want to see you next time.

The gift of listening

Let's face it. In the sales profession, we seem to get a bad rap from those outside of our industry. There are a multitude of reasons for this, but I think that top of the list is that we sometimes have a tendency to talk more than we listen when we meet with customers and prospects. But, this goes beyond listening skills. It is also the critical thinking at which we need to be successful. Anticipating questions, objections, and being able to think on our feet are all key attributes to being successful.

Sometimes we have such great knowledge about our product and services that we have great enthusiasm, and we want to share it with everybody even when they don't ask us specifically about it. The risk that we run is that we are showing the prospect or customer that we are not empathetic to their needs. We are taking a one-size-fits-all approach, and we also can waste the customer's time as a result of this.

What are some of the ways we can be the better listeners on our appointments? One idea is pre-call planning. When I was in medical sales, we had a coaching worksheet that my sales director and I would complete before the appointments when we worked together. It was also something we would use with new hires and field trainers as well. The thing I liked about the coaching worksheet is that it gave an opportunity to do some pre-call planning so that the meeting was tight. There was some firm objectives laid out and we didn't run the risk of coming unprepared or being inclined to just talk about our products.

Another idea is to prepare an agenda for important meetings, so that you stay focused and on task, especially if you're going to meet with an executive or one of your account key sponsors. In my years of sales, I found that most executives and decision-makers or account contacts really appreciated the agenda. It also gave them an opportunity to comment if there was anything that we left off. This was a great way to guarantee pre-call planning to get us on the right track before the meeting and to ensure that the meeting stayed focused and on time. Overall, I believe it showed that we cared, and not just about the meeting, but because we took the time to prepare in advance.

Last but not least, be flexible. I remember once my director and I were going into a very important meeting asking for a commitment from the customer to move forward with an opportunity for the end of our fiscal year. We had a prepared an agenda for the meeting and were ready to discuss our proposal. When we came into the meeting, to our dismay, the customer began telling us how upset they were with the performance of one of our products at one of their hospitals. They were also upset about one of the agreements they felt we had not executed in their original contract.

Needless to say, we were both taken by surprise. However, because we were flexible, focused, and emotionally grounded, we were able to answer the customer's challenges, and we were able to circle the meeting back to our proposal towards the end. We later made the sale, too.

**Helping your prospects to see what they don't —
Selling your insights, not your products**

Part of being a trusted advisor is to build credibility with your prospects. This means that you are looking out for their best interests by delivering unique insights and helping them avoid making a bad decision that could end up costing them a lot of money in the end. 'We are the experts so we should act like it,' said one of my mentors, my sales vice president. He had a customer challenge him with that once. Customers are waiting for us to advise them. It's no longer about just selling a product or service. It's about being a trusted advisor who is up-to-date on industry trends and with unique insights that help them avoid potential landmines and pitfalls. We are tasked today with looking out for our customers.

I was once challenged by my director of sales to close a sale in a hospital account by the end of the quarter, but the catch was I had not worked the deal and had no relationships or understanding of the *why* (the reason the customer needed my solution). I began the discovery process meeting with key stakeholders, and I soon found out there was a risk. One unit of the hospital had equipment with infusion safety software, my product, but the rest of the hospital had a competitive infusion equipment, which had been recalled. Without safety software, the competitive infusion equipment could potentially put the patients' care at risk. They were also not meeting certain regulatory requirements for pain management and care standards established by their governing organization, something that I could help them meet.

I shared my insights with the sponsor. At first she was not pleased, concerned I was sharing this risk or let's say 'insight' with other people in the hospital to make her look bad. But, soon she realized I was right and that my intent was not to damage her credibility. She came to understand that my role is as a medication safety consultant, and that there was a patient safety risk that needed to be addressed. I closed the sale 21 days later — a purchase order for $500K — initially a sale that looked impossible but became reality due to unique insights I provided.

Becoming a trusted advisor

Providing industry insights positions you as an advisor, consultant, and expert in your area, as we just discussed. So how can you be a trusted advisor? You may say 'I am new and I just don't know as much as I should about the industry I am selling in.' First of all, you do have credibility, and you've got to share that to 'earn the right' with the customer or prospect. Maybe 'I have been working in the X industry for X years, or I am an expert in X; I have the following credentials...' Chances are, no matter how new you are to your industry, company, product, or service, there is some unique skill or credential you are bringing to the table. Let the customer or prospect know about it at your initial meeting.

If you still need more credibility, there are many places you can go, including the Internet, tradeshows, professional organizations, your current customers who can educate you, your peers that may know the industry better than you, community leaders, conferences, community forums, the list goes on. Industry magazines, blogs, newsletters, and other publications are all a good source of industry insights. Also, your current customers are a safe place to learn. They would probably appreciate your asking them to show you their processes behind the scenes or just asking if you can come in one day to interview them or shadow them and learn more about their business, and the biggest challenges they face.

How to be different than the last competitor that came in the door

Bring value to the customer first, then the product. Be careful as to how you show up and present yourself to your prospect. Confidence is good, but arrogance is not. You never get a second chance to make a first impression. You don't want to be like the competitor that just came in the door, either.

I remember once I was working a competitive opportunity. The customer made some comments to me about how a competitor came into their account for their presentation. She told me that a group from this company was arrogant. They told her that she was 'making a mistake if her organization went forward with my or the other competitive product.' She said they also had an attitude as though they were strong-arming her organization into making a decision to purchase their products. She said there were 'many people standing in the presentation all wearing suits.'

I have to admit even now I got a chuckle inside of myself from hearing that the competition blew their opportunity. I also felt embarrassed for this other company and the way that they had presented themselves. I made a vow to myself that I never wanted anyone to think of me, or my company, in that same manner after hearing her story. Confidence is good, but humility is critical; would you buy from you?

Delivering a roadmap

From one of my sales vice-presidents, I learned the importance of helping to develop a roadmap for your customer. Again, instead of focusing on presenting just the product to your customer in addition to providing insights, you can differentiate yourself and bring value by helping them see their current state, and getting them to see the vision for their future state. Again, in order to do this, it's critical that you have an understanding of your customer's current challenges — their 'current state' — through the proper discovery that you have done in the sales process. Once you have done that discovery, you have the right to present a roadmap for the future for the customer. You can now paint a vision of the 'future or desired state.'

One of the best ways I have found to deliver a roadmap to the customer is through drawing a whiteboard. A whiteboard is a great conversation starter. A whiteboard is a drawing you provide showing your customer's current vs their desired state. It can help you avoid making the mistake of death by PowerPoint. The thing that is very unique about a whiteboard is that it is like a blank canvas. You can use your creativity or industry insights, and your knowledge of the current state of the customer to draw a picture of what their future could possibly look like.

Most of my best successes and sales have been through delivering a whiteboard. I have used whiteboards in my C Suite meetings. I've used a whiteboard for my final presentation to the committee — and won the sale. I can also say that I never saw my competitors draw a whiteboard in the sales process. If you don't know what to draw on your whiteboard, you can work with your marketing department to see if they can help to create some initial messaging that will show what your solution can do to help the customer achieve their future vision. Another great thing about a whiteboard is the customer will never know if you missed any parts of it. You know it better than anyone else, and no two whiteboards are the same!

Chapter 5
WHY SHOULD I BUY FROM YOU?

> Hold yourself responsible for a higher standard than
> anybody else expects from you.
> — HENRY WARD BEECHER

People buy from whom they like

It's no secret that people buy from whom they like. Let's take this outside of the product or service you are selling for a moment. Think about the last large purchase that you made in your life. Was it a home, a car, a boat? Was it some other type of service such as life insurance, finding an attorney or some type of professional advisor? When you made a decision to buy that product or to partner with some type of special service provider, I'm sure part of the reason that you agreed to go forward with that person was that you felt comfortable with their behavior style. Ask yourself 'Was it someone that I can relate to?' Most likely, the answer to the question is yes.

It goes beyond 'liking' someone, but much deeper to 'Am I comfortable with that person?' Do you trust the person? If you establish trust with the other person, whether you are the buyer or seller, it is easier to connect and influence each other on a deeper level. We can understand and relate to each other. We are naturally more inclined to want to be with someone else when there is trust and a deep level of connection. This is the secret to influencing someone else to buy from you.

Now think of someone who tried to sell you something that you did not buy. How was the experience for you? Did you feel anxiety with the other person? Did you feel as though you could not relate to that person and not trust them? Did you feel as though you had nothing in common? I would venture to guess that the answer to these questions was probably yes.

I can think of two times in my life when I went car shopping, for example. In the first instance, I felt a connection with the sales person. We had similar interests, laughed at the same things, and overall related to each other very well. We even went to the same high school.

With the second car buying experience, I didn't feel as though I could relate to the salesperson very well. He seemed more focused on making the sale than on getting to know me personally. We had different backgrounds. I don't remember us talking about any common interests. When I raised objections about the price, he did not show genuine care or concern that he wanted to work with me or negotiate. I bought a car in the first example but did not buy a car in the second example.

First of all, building a connection with someone else has to do with building rapport. But secondly, it has to do with understanding your personal behavior style and also being able to understand the behavior style of the person that we are meeting with. A key to success is being able to adjust our behavior style to make the other person feel comfortable during our meeting and interaction.

What's your style?

There are different behavior styles and many different surveys or analysis you can take to understand what your personal style is. I think of it as 'birds of a feather flock together.' Like birds, there are different behavior styles and images. Think of an eagle, a peacock, an owl, and a dove. Eagles like power; peacocks like recognition; owls like data and information; doves like support. Let's discuss these styles in further detail.

First of all, the eagle. The eagle likes power, control, and authority. They don't like to waste time on idle chitchat and prefer to get right down to business. They prefer to give the orders, not receive them.

They like a direct and fast pace. They are easily bored with details and don't want to get bogged down with too much information. Their key driver is power.

Second, the peacock. Peacocks like recognition and being the center of attention. They like to talk and socialize before they get down to business. They like social interaction, fast pace, and getting recognition for their efforts and accomplishments. They can become distracted or tune out with too many details. They may forget important information because they are busy socializing. Their key driver is social interaction.

Third, the owl. Owls like information and respect. They like to understand the details so that they can just get the job done. They are good at following a process. They like to be involved with processes that have a defined order. They like to move at a slower or moderate pace to be sure the job is done right and thoroughly. They prefer details and facts to people and socializing. They also like to ask questions. Their preference is information and data.

Fourth, the dove. Doves like people and support. They like to ensure that there is a general consensus and agreement with a group of people to get the job done. They are also good at teamwork and make great team players. They like to be involved with projects that involve collaboration and sharing of ideas. They like to move at a moderate pace and want to ensure that people are in agreement on a project. They prefer harmonious relationships. Their preference is people and teamwork.

Secrets to influencing the buyer behavior

Here are some ideas as to how you can influence a buyer. First, you have to understand their style. Now that you know about the different behavior styles, it can be easy to identify whom you are working with quickly. For example, if you are working with an eagle, let them feel as though they are in control. Stick to your agenda, and don't waste their time. When you are working with a peacock, let them share and talk more than you. Help them feel special like they are the center of attention. When you are working with an owl, make sure that you have brought facts and data to support the claims that you are making. Don't talk too fast, and be sure to give them respect throughout your meeting. While working with a dove, focus on teamwork, consensus of the group, and the value of collaborating. Handle conflict with care. Show them support for their ideas and don't talk too fast.

The bottom line is that, in order to build rapport and help others to build trust, they must feel comfortable with you. This means you must adapt to their style — especially if it is different than your own style!

How can I determine the buyer's style? — How to quickly identify the clues

The different behavior styles do have some similarities. For instance, both the eagle and the peacock will direct others/tell more than they will ask. However, the dove and the owl will ask more than they will direct others/tell. The eagle and the peacock tend to move and talk faster than the dove and the owl. The owl and the dove move at a slower, more methodical pace than the eagle and the peacock. If you go into an eagle's office, you will probably see trophies, certificates of recognition, and many awards. If you go into a peacock's office, you will probably see a lot of pictures of people, family, friends, and social gatherings. If you are in an owl's office, you may see books, statistics, data and abstract information. In the dove's office, you would probably see pictures of teams, people accomplishing great things together, and happy that they did so. The eagle and the owl are both focused on tasks. The peacock and the dove are more focused on people.

Lessons learned

I think we can all agree that in the sales profession, we are going to interact with many different behavior styles. The key to success is to know your style, be able to quickly identify the prospect or customer's style, and to help them feel comfortable by adapting to their style. Here are two examples; one where I failed to adapt and another where I was successful in adapting to the other person's style. They both had very different outcomes.

In one sales opportunity, I had a meeting with a prospect that got cancelled due to her having a sick child at home. I thought, 'Since I already made the trip, maybe I can see who else can meet with me in the hospital.' At the time, it seemed like a harmless decision. After meeting a couple contacts, I thought the day went well. As I was driving home, my phone rang, and it was the director of materials management. He was upset that I had not followed the hospital rules; 'drop by' appointments were prohibited. I was also told that I had failed to read the hospital vendor policy, and that I shouldn't come back again. It went downhill from there. I attempted to defend myself stating, 'I didn't know the rules.' He did not appreciate that. My boss ended up having to go back to the account, and I later figured out I was dealing with an 'eagle' who wanted to be in control. To him, I had violated his power.

By contrast, I experienced a different outcome early in my medical capital sales career. When I made my first big sale, there was a Chief Nursing Officer/Chief Operating Officer that I built a relationship and long term partnership with. We had a natural flow to our conversation and an instant rapport. I didn't have to filter what I would say, and we both were very outgoing and jovial in our conversations. I figured out that we both had the 'peacock' in our personality. He was comfortable with me meeting other key stakeholders and directed them to meet with me. He also shared with some of the other key decision makers in the other network hospitals the value he saw in our partnership and the outcomes we helped him achieve in quality and safety improvement. We had established a relationship because it was built on trust vs. opposition.

Chapter 6
PRESENT TO IMPRESS

Concerning all acts of initiative and creation, there is one
elementary truth - that the moment one definitely commits
oneself, the Providence moves, too.
— JOHANN WOLFGANG VON GOETHE

What are our top fears?

If I ask 'What are your top fears?' the typical
responses I get are: death, public speaking, snakes,
spiders, and heights. I looked up the 'top fears'
online, and that is exactly what came up! In this
chapter, we will talk about the thing we fear almost
as much as death: public speaking. But why do we
fear public speaking so much? It is almost as though,
when we stand up in front of a room, we are focused
on the worst thing that could happen, instead of how
we could succeed and win the crowd over. There are
many reasons that people are afraid of public
speaking. Amongst the top reasons are the
following; we are afraid that people will reject us, we
are afraid that people will reject our ideas, and that
people simply will not like us at all.

In this chapter, I'm going to share some ideas as to
how you can be a better presenter. But before you
get up to give your presentation, one critical thing to

think about is that you must look the part. Did you know that when you stand up in front of the group to speak or give a formal presentation, within the first 30 seconds of your talk people are already making judgments about your social class, income, and educational status by the way you present yourself and dress?

The good news is that one of the easiest things you can do is give a professional impression. In other words, dress and groom yourself to have an impact on your audience. When I was at a Toastmasters contest a couple years ago, there was an individual who was going to compete at the division level. He showed up in a pair of grungy jeans and a beat-up looking shirt. I was surprised to see this, thinking he may have wanted to present himself better to give the judges and audience a stronger impression of himself. One of my favorite sayings is 'You need to dress up to the level that you want to be.' I also think of it as though you want to look the part and in some way gain the respect of the audience by the way that you appear.

Now of course, there may be some instances where dressing professionally may not be appropriate for your audience. For example, when Steve Jobs made his presentations at Apple, he often wore jeans and a black shirt. Certain regions of the country may dress more formally than others. For instance, when I had meetings in Chicago, I dressed up, because that was the culture in the hospitals I called on. But when I was in a remote rural area of Illinois, dressing up too much would put people off. When I was in operating room sales, it was important to dress down and minimize the jewelry. When I did clinical walkthrough assessments at hospitals, it was important to dress down as we didn't want the nursing staff to think we were state inspectors wearing suits and carrying clipboards.

Most of my sales presentations were in front of hospital or business committees, and I always dressed up, wearing a business suit for the majority of my professional career. It's something that I made a habit and got used to. I would think to myself that I was asking people to spend hundreds, thousands, or even millions of dollars for my product or service, and it was up to me to show that I cared enough to look professional. Not to mention, you never know whom you may run into. There were many times that I would run into a hospital or business executive that I did not expect to, in a hallway, or even on an elevator, and I am thankful that I did look the part.

The last piece of advice is, if you are inviting other sales team or support team members to present with you or do a product demonstration with you, make sure to let them know what the dress code is going to be; whether it's business casual or something else. I once had a product demonstration day, and everyone was dressed professionally except one person who decided to show up in casual dress, crop pants, and a short-sleeved top. I remember wondering if they were going to go change their clothes. I admit I was accountable because I hadn't told everyone to dress up. It was awkward, and I learned to always mention the dress code when I was planning with my support team after that experience!

What can I do to be the best presenter when I hate public speaking?

I found out the hard way that if you want to get the advance in the sale you want, you need to be an awesome presenter. Early in my career, I had the opportunity to present to a C-Suite executive team of a hospital health system. My role was to simply introduce my sales leadership and strategic account VP, who would do the majority of the presentation. It was the opportunity I had dreamed of, that could result in a $6M sale if we were lucky to have the customer make a decision to partner with us. The days and hours leading up to the presentation, I secretly wished I had never volunteered to do the introduction and share with the hospital executive team the discovery that had been done. I wished I had never shared how our company and solution was best positioned to be a future business partner of this 6-hospital health system.

The morning of the presentation, I was so nervous I felt sick to my stomach. Then the moment came. I stood up, gave my introduction, which ended up being about 3 sentences vs. the 5 minute intro I had prepared. I felt like I was in a black hole, and I don't remember what I said. But, I remember one thing. I sat down and felt humiliated and angry with myself. But, I also became inspired and motivated to become a better speaker. 'That's it, I thought — I have to get better at public speaking!' I joined Toastmasters and today, 7 years later, I am still involved. I can honestly say not only did I overcome my fear of public speaking, I became a better and more confident leader.

The good news is that we did get the sale, and I learned a lesson. You've got to present to impress. You never know whom you will be in front of when duty calls! As I advanced from this experience, not only did my sales improve, but presenting to groups became one of my 'favorite things.' It also became a road to helping me move into a Sales Trainer role, which requires me to constantly be speaking in front of groups.

Secrets of top presenters

In addition to giving many sales presentations over the years, I was also an avid member of Toastmasters International, and have been a member for the past seven years. I am one of the 5% of Toastmasters who achieved the Distinguished Toastmaster Award (DTM), so I guess you can say I am pretty passionate about Toastmasters! There are 10 key lessons I learned about how to be a top presenter. Here is my "Secrets to Top Presenters" list:

Have a point. If you remember just one thing about public speaking remember this: Have a point. All too often speaker's stand up in front of an audience and blabber out one long stream of consciousness, product features, or benefits. What is the point or the goal of your speech? Do you want to influence your audience? Do you want to sell them something or ask them to take action? Know your goal and build your presentation around it.

Have an introduction, body, and conclusion. Follow the age-old advice, "Tell them what you are going to tell them, tell them, and then tell them what you told them." Most people find writing the body first is most helpful, then either the introduction or the conclusion.

Prepare. Practice makes prepared! You cannot "over-prepare". The better you know the material, the more confident you will be when presenting, and the more flowing the presentation or speech will sound. Videotape or record yourself if possible, or at least rehearse by watching yourself in a mirror. When you are delivering your talk live, the same adrenaline that makes you nervous also helps you think better and help to find the right words to make your speech sound fluent.

Have good eye contact. If you have been taught to look over the heads of those you are speaking to, forget it. Good eye contact means making a connection with your audience by looking them straight in the eyes. If the audience is small enough, try to make it a point to make eye contact with everyone.

Anticipate questions. Take the time to think about any question a listener may ask and formulate a positive answer that supports your presentation. It is okay to say you do not know the answer and tell the person you will get back to them if needed. The

"I don't know" or "I can't say" answers are most effective when followed by "but I'll tell you what I do know..."

Try to keep your speech less than 20 minutes. Several studies have shown that 20 minutes is about the maximum amount of time listeners can stay attentive. After that, the attention levels begin to drop. Speaking is more stimulating than listening so although you may be excited to talk longer, the chances are your listeners are ready for a break.

Establish credibility. Who are you to speak about the subject you are speaking of? Why should your audience listen to you? Establish your credibility by sharing your credentials with the listeners in a tactful way up front at the start of your talk.

Have a strong introduction and a strong conclusion. The introduction should be used to gain the attention of the listeners and persuade them to listen to your entire presentation. You are essentially selling them on why they should listen. Be sure you address their needs and not yours. Ask a question or tell a personal story to gain the audience's attention. The conclusion should consist of a powerful statement, quotation, anecdote, call-to-action, or other attention-grabber. Never end a speech with "that's all."

Act on every opportunity you can to speak. Anxiety of speaking is best subsided by experience. Also, volunteering to be the one who gives the speech will get you noticed and you will stand out as the leader. Join your local Toastmasters club (www.toastmasters.org) for some really great practice.

The Power of the Pause. If you lose your place, pause and re-collect yourself. Don't apologize to the audience! Replace "um" an "uh" with a pause. Before and during your speech, breathe. Visualize the outcome you want. They probably don't know, and you know your material better than anyone. Smile, Relax, and Have Fun! Your audience will be more at ease if you are.

The top mistakes to avoid during a presentation

In my many years of giving sales presentations, Toastmaster speeches, competing at Toastmasters contests, sales training, and other speaking engagements, I can say I have learned what not to do! First of all, ignoring the list that I just presented would be one thing not to do! I want to share with you now some of the learnable moments that either I experienced personally or I've seen other presenters make that have gotten their presentation off to a bad start or have left them with a not-so-favorable impression on the audience.

Not arriving early or showing up late. Nothing gets a presentation off to a worse start if you are late or you haven't given yourself enough time to set up. If you are late, your credibility is instantly damaged. It's important to arrive early to check out the room, the speaking area, and also to help give yourself a few minutes to compose your mind before you talk.

Getting into a confrontation with an audience member. Yes, our worst nightmare is the audience member who is confrontational or objects to what we are saying. If this happens to you, respect the person who is confronting you, and calmly (even if you are irritated) tell them they are making a good point. Ask them if you can take the conversation off-line after the meeting. But getting into an argument is going to derail your presentation and also make you lose control of the room. I once had a sales manager that got into an argument with an audience member, and it was not only awkward, it gave the customer a bad impression of our company.

Forgetting to do your AV check before your presentation. If you are going to have AV or a projector in your presentation, this is another reason to show up very early. Have a backup plan in place in case there is an AV disaster. This once happened to me in a hospital presentation. The projector did not work for the entire presentation, and thankfully I knew my products and my presentation well enough that I didn't need the projector.

Not speaking loud enough or talking too fast. Speaking loud keeps your audience's attention. If you have a soft voice, practice speaking louder or use a microphone if you must. Also, speaking too fast is very difficult for an audience to follow. This is a common issue when we are nervous. Again, join Toastmasters so that you can practice your public speaking in a safe non-threatening environment if this is an issue for you.

Death by PowerPoint. If you must use PowerPoint for your presentation, keep one single idea on the slide. Also remember if you have 30 minutes for a presentation, you better not come in with 30 slides. You need to allow extra time for questions and conversation. A great alternative to PowerPoint is whiteboarding or flip-charting your ideas for the audience.

Not finding out in advance who is going to be in the audience. It is critical to understand who your audience is going to be, especially if you are giving a business or sales presentation. The content of your presentation may be relevant to some audience members but not to others. I remember once I was going to give a presentation to a group that I thought was going to be hospital executives, and it ended up being staff nurses. Needless to say, the presentation I prepared was for the wrong audience. Don't let this happen to you!

Answering too many questions during your presentation. We all know that the audience is going to have questions about what you are presenting. The challenge is if you have a limited time for your talk, the time you spend answering questions can take away from your valuable presentation time. When I give timed presentations, I always let the audience know that I will take questions at the end of my presentation so that we don't lose time or getting derailed by side conversation. I've always built some extra time at the end for Q and A.

Giving out handouts at the beginning of your talk. Giving too many handouts or pieces of literature about your product or service at the beginning of the presentation can be a distraction for your audience and take attention away from your talk. The only time that I give out handouts during a presentation is if it is a worksheet that people will be filling in or taking notes on such as for a sales training class. Other handouts should be given after your talk is over.

Not being prepared if a co-presenter does not show up. If you are presenting with someone else, it is important that you know their material as well as your own. In my years of sales training, I have had presenters cancel, have a flat tire, get sick, etc. at the last minute, and I ended up having to present their material. Thankfully I was prepared, and it didn't turn into a disaster.

Telling the audience if you make a mistake or if it's your first time presenting this subject. If you make a mistake while you are presenting don't say anything about it. It only draws attention to the mistake that you just made, and chances are the audience didn't even notice it until you said something about it. Also, I have heard presenters say, "This is the first time that I am presenting this material." Even though that may be the truth, people probably don't care. Don't reveal that to the audience because it creates a sense of awkwardness, and it also hurts your credibility at the start of your talk. You can always tell the audience afterwards, and they will probably tell you that you did a great job!

Email dos and don'ts

I think that we can all agree we live in the new world of email communication. Of course, the benefits of email are that you can quickly communicate with people, keep in touch with colleagues, internal/external customers, do your prospecting, and communicate with multiple team members and people at one time. But, with the benefits also come some challenges that we sometimes create for ourselves through email. I have learned many lessons about email that I'm sure you will agree with:

Know when to pick up the phone. Sometimes email is just not the right place for communication. Some instances are when emotions are running high. When emotions run high, intelligence runs low. I think we have all been in a situation when we have replied to email when the emotional stakes were high, and then we later regretted what we sent to the other person. Furthermore, we may hit 'reply' to someone else who was angry and our words on the email are misinterpreted, which can leave them even angrier. Another time not to use email is if you are delivering information that is sensitive. For instance, having to give someone else feedback about their performance. I always appreciated if a customer called me personally to let me know I had not won the business versus sending me an email. I have heard stories of people getting terminated or released from a company through email. I personally don't agree with that.

Be careful of the "reply all" syndrome. Sometimes there is a string of email, and there are many people who are copied even though the subject really does not have anything to do with them. I think these end up creating more confusion, and can also open you up for more unnecessary responses and feedback. Also, be very careful if a customer is copied on a company and internal email and there is sensitive information being discussed. Once I saw a sales manager reply all on an email that a customer was copied, and the manager was giving some negative feedback about the delay in our internal processes. Once we hit the send button it's too late!

Be mindful of after-hours emails. Some companies have policies that state that you are not responsible for answering emails after business hours or on weekends. Let's face it. If you are traveling or working on a big deal that is about to close, you probably will be spending time on email after hours and even weekends. But if you are trying to avoid being on email after hours or on weekends, make sure that you are not the one initiating the emails. If people send you emails after hours or on weekends, the more you respond, the more you are sending them the message that it is okay for them to do that and that you will answer.

Voice Mail Tips

WIIFM? What's in it for me? Why should they call you back? In other words, give the person a reason why they would want to call you back. Help them be curious about what you want to share with them. For example, 'I would love to share an idea that will help save your organization $100,000/year;' instead of 'I want to talk to you about my product and service.' Not only is that boring, it sounds like every other sales representative out there! Don't be average — be exciting with your voice messages.

Be upfront and brief about the purpose of the message. Avoid story telling and get to the point. People decide within seconds if they want to listen to you or your message. We all know people's time and attention spans can be limited, especially if they are a key decision-maker or executive. They probably have many voicemails to listen to in addition to yours. The goal is to get someone to return your call!

Be enthusiastic and positive in your tone, while using authority. People like to connect and engage with others who are positive. Being assertive is also another way to establish you as an authority and someone that people want to connect and do business with. Smile while you are talking. Keep a mirror on your desk so you can see yourself while you speak.

Be clear about what you are asking the person on the other end to do. Do you want them to call you, email you, or do something else? What action are you asking them to take on your behalf? Don't forget to say that in your message.

Leave important information clearly and say it slowly. If you want someone to call you back and they can't understand you or you are talking too fast, that won't happen! I usually repeat my phone number when I leave important voice messages. With today's technology, the good news is you can usually play back the message you left to ensure it is clear, concise, and easily understood. I advise you do it. Personally, I have received voice messages where, even after replaying them a few times, I still cannot understand the person's name, phone number, or where they are calling. Mumbling is not a good idea on voice mail. Don't cut off the chance of someone calling you back because you left a poor quality message.

Set the callback times. If you are asking someone to call you back, let him or her know when you are free to take his or her call. This gives the impression that you are busy and your time is limited. If you are setting an appointment, give the person two or three days/times you can meet. This helps avoid 'phone tag' of leaving messages back and forth and also shows you are a busy professional taking care of other customers.

Chapter 7
NEGOTIATING FOR A WIN-WIN AND COMMITMENT TO THE CLOSE

Obstacles are things a person sees when he takes his eyes
off his goal.
— JOSEPH COSSMAN

Negotiation before, during, and after the sale

When it comes to negotiating, I think there is a misunderstanding that only happens when we are giving the customer the proposal or pricing quote. In my experience, negotiation is happening throughout the sales process. The customer may ask you for a demonstration on short notice at the start of the sales cycle. They may ask you for discounts before you give them the first quote. Then, when you give the quote there may be more pricing concession requests. But what about after you get the order? Yes, you may still be negotiating then. Here is an example:

There was a particular sale that I closed one year that I will never forget. For starters, I needed this opportunity to close to make my annual sales quota number. It had been one of the worst sales performance years of my career. Yes, the stakes were high, but my team also needed the win, along with my sales director and vice-president. To make matters worse, there were two days of the fiscal year left. The customer, after much persuasion, agreed to sign all of the agreements and issue the purchase order in time for the year-end close. It all came in at 3 PM on the last day of the fiscal year.

As I was getting ready to celebrate the win and the year being over, I realized that the customer had forgotten to sign 1 more document. It was an agreement that the customer would also buy the consumable products that went with my equipment. We had given a large order discount contingent upon this missing document also being signed. I had to go and meet the customer about this. My Director gave me some of the best negotiating advice I have heard and was critical to this moment: Don't Flinch — also translated as 'Use Your Power.'

I calmly reminded the customer of the commitment they made, and the discount was contingent upon that. He initially pushed back on me saying he would get penalized from the current consumables vendor if he signed the agreement for consumable products from my company. I again repeated our initial agreement and told him I would help him get through this. But, I needed him to stick to our original agreement. He signed the agreement and I learned a valuable lesson — don't give away your power, even when someone is trying to break an agreement.

The key principles of negotiation

Position your product/service in a way that is advantageous. This means to describe your products/services in a compelling way that clearly conveys their value. Since value is subjective, the manner in which you position your products and services almost always affects their perceived value. Keep it brief, compelling and often repeated.

Set high targets. In sales negotiation, those who ask for more typically get more, and those with low targets typically get less and under-achieve. Those who ask for more reinforce a high-value position for their product in the customer's mind. Many salespeople fail to set high targets because they have low aspirations. This is either because they are afraid to negotiate or because they don't feel confident overcoming price objections. This results in a customer's perception of value being low.

Manage information carefully. Many sales negotiators 'leave money on the table' because they share sensitive information on price flexibility, internal deadlines, and free extras with their customers at the wrong time. Others feel this makes them appear responsive to their customers' requests for data and dump too much information on the table early in the sales process. Skilled professionals carefully plan a strategy for giving and getting information during sales negotiations.

Know the full range and strength of your power. Negotiations are about power. Negotiation power can be used to form mutually advantageous agreements or it can be used to intimidate and bully. In order to utilize power effectively in negotiation, you must (1) understand the source of power available to you and (2) maintain your power under the stress of dealing with parties whose perceptions and/or goals are in conflict with yours. Most negotiators underestimate their power.

Satisfy customer needs over wants. Needs are urgent. Wants are very particular and narrow. There are not many ways (maybe one or two) to satisfy wants, whereas the creative possibilities for satisfying uncovered needs are limitless.

Concede according to plan. Many salespeople give away too much, too soon, and too quickly. Sometimes they lack confidence and negotiation skills. They are uncomfortable with the tension of the sales process. Related symptoms of weak sales negotiating are giving away valuable price concessions without getting anything in return. Top sale professionals know instinctively that a key to profitable negotiating is to concede slowly and reluctantly and to get something of value in return for a concession.

Keys to dealing with price pressure

- Lead with value and position around value
- Compare value, not price
- Build negotiating space into your proposals — You are better off to start high vs. too low. Don't start at the lowest point
- Concede slowly and reluctantly
- Exchange price concessions for true commitment
- Avoid negotiating on price alone (What else can you offer the customer that doesn't cost your company much but brings them value? e.g. – delivery, installation, invoicing dates)
- Get to the real business need – Why is the prospect asking for the discount or price concession?

- Uncover the underlying personal needs which would be met by a price concession, and work to meet them
- Uncover the whole rationale for the price/discount request
- Use 'limited authority' (For example, 'I need to get my boss's approval before I can offer you a discount .' This buys you time.)

The top mistakes to avoid during negotiations

When we negotiate, the stakes are higher for both the buyer and the seller. These are some of the common mistakes I have seen and experienced during negotiations:

- Focusing on price
- Giving a concession (e.g. – discount, extended terms) and not getting something in return
- Overconfidence — 'If I give this, I will make the sale'
- Sharing too much information with the prospect
- When faced with an objection, giving more information than what was asked — not answering the objection
- Giving up your power

- Being afraid of prolonged silence – Get comfortable with silence and tension
- Not saying *no* to unreasonable requests
- Getting stuck on features and benefits versus what is important to the prospect
- Not allowing enough room in your proposal for negotiation space
- Adding extra products or services to the proposal that the customer does not see value in

Making demands — What do I say?

During negotiations, it is important that we own our power. This also means that there will be times when we must make demands to the prospect. I know you are probably thinking 'Wait, I thought the prospect was making demands on us during the negotiation?' Even know it may seem as though the prospect is making demands during negotiations, one way to remain in control and to own your power is for you to make demands on the prospect. Here are some examples of that by answering their demand in the form of a question:

Prospect: Your price is too expensive.
Sales Rep: When you say expensive, what do you mean by that?

Prospect: I need my boss to approve this before I can move forward. I will get back to you.
Sales Rep: Great! Why don't we set up a meeting with you and your boss so that we can move forward?

Prospect: I'm sorry, but I can't sign off on the paper work even with the discount that you already gave me.
Sales Rep: We made an agreement that if I gave you the discount, you would be able to move forward. I need you to keep to our agreement. What will you need to do to honor our agreement?

Prospect: We like our current supplier; I don't think we can move forward with you.
Sales Rep: I can certainly understand and appreciate that. If there were anything that you could change about the way that your current supplier is doing business with you, what would it be?

There is one more concept to consider during negotiations. I call it the ice cream cone method. That means that when your prospect is asking you for concessions or discounts, it is important that, as you continue to give concessions or discounts, they get smaller and smaller throughout the process. Giving larger discounts or concessions as the negotiation process continues sends a message to your prospect that they are being rewarded for asking for more discounts.

Objections are questions in disguise

One of a salesperson's biggest fears is handling objections. But if you think of an objection as being a question in disguise, it is much easier to handle, and simply answering a question will not keep you from making the sale. If you think about it, people would not raise objections with you if they were not interested in what you have to offer. Therefore, objections are a good sign. Here are some keys to handling objections:

- Don't give more information than what is being 'asked' in the objection. It is common in sales to do a feature/benefit dump when someone simply just needs more information.
- Be comfortable with silence. When you ask a question, wait seven seconds for the answer.
- If you don't ask, the answer is always *no*.
- If you do not understand an objection, ask clarifying questions, instead of providing an answer that the prospect does not care about.
- If you cannot answer the objection or the question, simply let the prospect know that

you need to get back to them instead of giving them the wrong answer or making a commitment that you cannot keep.

- If the objection involves multiple people at the account, ask if you can meet with the other parties if that is necessary vs. having a middle man that could confuse the information or your responses.
- Answer an objection with a question. For example, 'your price is too high' could be answered with 'when you say too high, what do you mean by that?'
- Show empathy and that you care about the objection, and stay focused and confident that you can handle it.

Chapter 8
TEAMWORK – IT'S THE TEAMWORK THAT WILL MAKE THE DREAM WORK

We will either find a way or make one.
— HANNIBAL

Together Everyone Achieves More – Even in the sales world

We have all heard the saying T.E.A.M. – Together Everyone Achieves More. There are many professions where teamwork is vital. If you look at sports teams, the airlines industry, restaurants, any type of service organization, they all rely on teamwork. I think one of the challenges and sales that we face is that we tend to think of ourselves as lone rangers. The risk in this is that we could be missing out on valuable support and insights from others, as well as opportunities to learn best practices.

Everybody loves a team player. Being a team player means that you give to others, without expecting something in return. I remember for the most part on my sales teams that everybody did want each other to succeed, and we were really only as strong as the weakest link. Yes, it was competitive, but we

95

all had each other's back. Once in a while, there would be a team member that was a lone ranger. The issue with this is that if you are the lone ranger and don't help others out, others won't be as inclined to help you out when you need it. And, you never know when you are going to need help. It always seems as though we need help at the last minute, as urgent customer requests come up often!

Keep this in mind if you are not showing up as a team player today; I encourage you to be a team player because it will make your life much easier and help you sell more. Teamwork is your secret weapon.

To be successful in the sales organization is a team effort. No matter how big or small of an organization you work for, it takes many people on the front lines as well as behind the scenes to help you win your business. Everyone from the marketing teams to customer service, the contracts department, the sales compensation department, and of course the entire field sales team all rely upon each other for success.

Through my years in sales, I would send thank-you notes to the support staff that helped me during the busy times, such as the end of the quarter or fiscal year. My sales team would pitch in and buy our contracts analyst a Christmas present or gift card each year end to thank her for the amount of work she would take on to help us close all of our quarterly or year-end contracts. She often worked after business hours and during weekends to complete all of our orders (which included multiple terms and conditions with dozens of pages that needed to be reviewed before we could book the order). My team would also get together and buy our sales director or manager a Christmas gift to thank them for their leadership and everything they did to help us be successful. Even something as simple as a handwritten thank-you card or note goes a long way!

What you bring to the team comes back to you

In my sales career, I always loved the sense of teamwork on my regional sales team. There were so many times that we would help each other out, no matter what the call of duty was. Everything from helping each other at presentations, loaning each other our demonstration equipment, sharing ideas with each other, sharing documents, and messaging we created to make us better against the competition. We would team up to go out and help a newer team member with a first demo, C Suite meeting, or committee presentation. Not to mention being there to provide moral support after a tough sales day or the loss of a key deal. All are examples of some of the things we did for each other as a team. As I look back, I always knew who I could count on to help me. And, I was always there to help them out as well. Sales is definitely not a do-it-yourself profession!

How to get others to work for you — not against you

One of the best ways to drive results is to treat other people as you want to be treated. This includes everyone on your internal team, no matter what level they are, as well as the contacts in your account. I have found that you never know where people will go or advance to. Also within certain industries, people travel in small circles. People also get promoted to decisions of power and decision-making authority. Making enemies or adversaries in any business or industry will not get you very far. In other words, don't burn your bridges!

Find a mentor, be a mentor

In my sales career, I always looked around at the people who were doing well. I would ask them if I could pick their brain to find out what they were doing that made them successful. I would constantly seek out mentors. Then when I got better and more experienced, I would offer to be a mentor to other new sales hires. I spent years as a sales field trainer. It was probably one of my favorite roles when I was in sales. Not only did I feel as though I was making a contribution to others professional and sales skills development, but it helped me to reinforce the best practices I needed to continue to do to be successful. Also I think that when people ask you for help, it gives you a sense of pride that you must be doing something right!

I am grateful for the mentors I had in my sales career. Some of the top mentors for me who stand out were my area vice-president and my director of sales. I remember the first time I worked with my area vice president. I was still fairly new in my medical capital sales position. I have not had much success yet. However, I felt like I was working my tail off. I felt unsure of myself because I didn't have any big wins just yet. He came out to work with me, and I will never forget his words of encouragement. He said 'You have everything it takes to be successful. Just keep doing what you are doing. I know that you are going to be a success based on what I saw today!' Not only did he give me the encouragement that I needed to hear, he let me know that what I was doing was the right activity. It meant the world to me. Sometimes encouragement is all it takes to get us to the next level. He was right. I closed my biggest sale months later while working with my area vice-president.

The other mentor that I am thankful for was the sales director I reported to. She taught me many things, but some of the things that stand out the most for me were the skill of critical thinking, being a challenger, and the ability to manage myself as well as take control of every situation, customer and challenge I faced with assertiveness and finesse. Because of the ability she had to hold me to a very high standard of excellence, I was able to take one of my most difficult sale years, being at 11% of my quota, and end my year at 117%, over-achieving my sales goal. She helped me to see that what was holding me back was a lack of focus and strategy to make my number. Once I got back on track with the best strategy, everything fell into place.

Of course, I have to thank my mom. When I first started out in business-to-business sales, she reminded me that sales and the activity of prospecting is a numbers game; in other words, it is not worth getting hung up and emotional when we hear the word 'no.' It is all part of the game. The more we prospect, track our activity, and do the activity, the better we get! She always reminded me to stay positive and have fun while doing the work it takes to be successful in sales! People do business with whom they like, trust, and appreciate.

Being the leader not the follower pays

As I look back on my 21+ year sales career, I have a confession. I cannot take credit on my own for every single win. It took mentors, many times my director/boss, sales leadership, internal resources, internal resident experts and subject matter experts, even clients and customers that were willing to be references for prospective sales opportunities. All of these teams of people helped me out on the front lines as well as behind the scenes. Many came from all over the US to support me. Why do I share this? In sales, it is a team sport, not an individual sport.

Yes, I know you are saying, 'But Amy, I have to make my number — I own it.' Yes, to some extent, that is true. But most of the top producers I have seen had sales mentors and teachers. And, when it comes to a sales team, we are only as strong as the weakest link. I often see reps who are struggling, who are ashamed, and don't want to ask for help because they think it is 'sign of weakness.' Or, they get caught up in 'woe is me' when things are not going right (refer back to the Accountability and Attitude Chapters for a refresh). Forget that — it takes humility and honesty to say 'I want to be more; how were you successful?'

How would I know this? Because I have been there. When I was new to sales, my mom, a fellow sales trainer, was my mentor. Whenever I hit a 'low point,' I reached out for help, even if it was to brainstorm. Put your pride on the back burner; why reinvent the wheel? Success leaves clues, so learn from the ones who have been a success!

Chapter 9
INVESTING IN YOURSELF

There are two primary choices in life: to accept conditions as they exist, or accept the responsibility for changing them.
— DENNIS WAITLEY

Being honest with yourself is the first step to being a sales rock star

In order to be a sales hero, it is an important that you are honest with yourself at all times. This means that, when you are not performing where you need to be or want to be, you've got to be able to ask yourself some tough questions. I still remember several years ago when I was having a very 'zero' sales performance year. I was on sales probation, and I had to ask myself the tough question: Do I want to stay in this sales profession or do I want to change what I'm doing to be a better performer?

Sometimes we are at a crossroads and it is necessary to decide what road we want to travel. We can't stay at the fork in the road in indecision. It is never easy to ask ourselves these types of questions, but when things aren't working, it's critical that we get clear about what is working and what is not working. I made the decision to 'change what I am doing to be a better performer,' which is the inspiration behind this book. I had to go 'back to the basics' and evaluate the fact I had not been doing the right activity to be successful. Essentially, I was not following the principles of this book. Also, my attitude was focused on 'what if I fail?' vs. 'how can I turn this around?' Once I decided it was time to refocus, everything fell into place. I went from being at 11% of my annual quota to 117% at year-end, and I doubled my income!

Being 'stuck' is a decision. When I feel 'stuck,' I ask myself 'What is causing me to feel this way?' It is usually an emotional focus. I am focusing on what is wrong, something that happened, or something I am denying I am responsible for (e.g. – poor sales performance). It is easy to stay in a rut if we let ourselves. But, this is not only detrimental to your attitude, it is poison to your sales results. Yes, we are human and with that come challenges and emotions. But, the key is to be aware of this and to stay in that place too long!

The power of self-development

I have personally invested thousands of dollars in self-development, motivational and leadership trainings, and personal coaching; not to mention the books, audio programs, and coaching programs I have invested my time and money in. Why do I do this? In my experience, we live in a world and an environment with many distractions, some of which can be negative and have a bad influence on us. I have developed unique insights, new perspectives and leadership skills, overcome my own personal challenges, and not to mention, learned valuable life lessons, as well as picked up some great tips on how to better present from being an audience member in front of top paid presenters!

I am not suggesting that you must go out and spend the same time and money I have invested since I was 19 years old, but what I am suggesting is to be open to new ideas, learning, and perspectives. I also appreciate the variety of people, new connections, and many great networking opportunities that I have come across as a result of live trainings, networking groups, and self-development organizations. Why reinvent the wheel or create something when an expert you can follow has already done that? Knowledge is everywhere...

I think of self-development as a journey of transformation. One of my favorite sayings is that excellence is a journey, not a destination. Lifespring was one of the first self-improvement programs I went through was when I was 19 years old, while I was a student at the University of Kansas. I believe that program was probably one of the most transformative experiences I ever went through. It helped change my life — for the better. It was at this workshop that I became aware of my self-limiting beliefs. I had survived a near-death experience at age 9. A drunken driver-related car accident that not only left me on the brink of death, but with a major head injury and facial trauma. My skull was fractured, re-wired back together with over 500 stitches in my face after the accident.

My family was told if I did survive, I might be blind, deaf, or brain damaged. Thankfully, I recovered without any of that. I had many reconstructive and cosmetic surgeries on my face from this near-death experience at a young age. I struggled with rebellion, low self-confidence, and a constant self-consciousness about my looks. As a result of that I became focused on what I looked like instead of what was the most important thing; what's on the inside, my character.

From going through the Lifespring program I learned that it's really not what is on the outside that is important, but it's our inner strength and courage; our determination and our inner power that makes us who we really are. I found out from that experience that what I really wanted to do in my lifetime was to make a contribution and make a difference for others. That experience really helped me tap into my true personal power and human potential. I realized that my mission was to share my determination and inspiration to succeed and overcome life challenges with everybody that I would come into contact with. I think that is why I am so committed to helping people make a difference and get better in their sales career, which in turn will help them succeed in their life.

Adding value to others' lives

I have heard it said that we are directly paid in proportion to the amount of value that we bring to other people's lives. The reason I mention that is because in order to be successful in sales, it takes two things. First you must care about other people and bringing value to them. Second, you must also be a leader and a natural influencer. Third, you must have enthusiasm about you and the product or service you are representing. The last four letters of enthusiasm are 'iasm' (I Am Sold Myself).

Being in the sales profession means that you automatically have the opportunity to bring value to other people's lives. Yes, it is your products and services that you're selling, but really it's also about the unique insights, perspectives, and knowledge you're providing to other people. Also, the fact that you are making their life and business better by what you are helping them acquire is a pretty big influence that you have on others!

Think of yourself as a change agent. Yes, you have the honor, and the privilege, to change someone else by what you are doing on a daily basis in your sales profession. For example, I remember when I was selling infusion safety systems to hospitals. The products eliminated medication errors and in turn made patient care safer not just for the nurse, but it also had the ability to save patients' lives.

I think my favorite part of that job was not as much about making the sale and the commissions as it was about being onsite at the hospital the day that we were installing the equipment to 'go live' on patients. I felt such a sense of gratitude and happiness knowing that the hospital was going to be safer as a result of the product that they had just installed and spent their capital dollars on. I knew that it was going to make healthcare safer, save lives, and protect both nurses and patients from unintended medication programming errors. I felt like I had truly made a difference.

Commit to being a lifelong learner — don't settle for mediocrity

Have you heard the saying that we are either growing or we are dying? Lifelong learning is about expanding outside of your comfort zone. It is about the ability to look within and ask yourself 'How can I take it to another level?' It's about being humble with yourself and never settling for being average or mediocre. It's about constantly pushing yourself to a new level. As result of constantly pushing yourself beyond what you think you are capable of, you get a huge reward. This huge reward is what I call breakthroughs. A great thing happens when we overcome self-limiting beliefs, stories, the past, or the reason why we think we cannot be successful at something. Once we've broken through that limiting belief or story, one of the biggest rewards is self-esteem, confidence, and personal conviction — a new beginning.

From being a lifelong learner, I was able to the fulfill one of my dreams — becoming a sales trainer. I had been in sales for over 21 years, and after serving as a sales field trainer and training new sales team members while I was a sales rep, the light bulb went on for me. I realized what I was really excited about was about teaching and training others to be better at their sales profession.

I wanted to share everything that I had learned — from the good times of being a top performer, as well as the many learnable moments when I was not performing where I needed to be and how I got better from those experiences. I was lucky to get promoted into a sales training manager position, and today my personal satisfaction comes when a new sales team member I trained calls me and tells me of a win that they had in the field. I also enjoy hearing them thank me for what I had taught and trained them on. When I do my one-on-one sales coaching, the win for me is when someone has a breakthrough or they realize what is keeping them from being successful in sales is only that self-limiting voice they have in their head.

There are no such things as mistakes — Only learnable moments

As I look back on my entire sales career, I know I learned a lot from the times when I was a top performer receiving sales awards, standing on stage at the national sales meeting, seeing my name in the sales rankings, and receiving congratulatory emails from my sales director and executive leaders in my sales organization. But, I have to confess that most of my major advances in my sales ability and results came from learnable moments; from the times when

I was not doing so well. Yes, I learned most from the times when I was not making sales, the times when I was having difficult discussions with my sales director, the one time when I was put on sales probation. Although those were very difficult times, I remember them very well because I had to look within myself, and it was 100% up to me to turn the situation around. I had to re-commit to excellence and once again prove to myself I already had everything I needed within myself.

My years of experience to succeed and overcome any obstacles had value during the tough times. Hence the saying if it's to be, it's up to me. It was during the challenging times that I had to go back to the basics. Really, everything that I've talked about in this entire book. It's really about following the principles that makes us a success in sales. It's not secrets or fancy formulas or techniques, in my experience. It is about being 100% focused on success, resourceful, and doing the work while working smart. When I wrote this book, I thought about everything I did to turn my most challenging times into success and what I did that helped me turn around my performance to go 'from a sales zero to a sales hero.' I always told myself that, if I could turn around my performance from the times I was feeling like a 'sales zero' under performing to a 'sales hero' over-achieving my sales quota, I would have an awesome story to tell others. Most importantly, I would share my keys to success with others to help them and make a difference.

I wish you the best of success, and that you never forget: you are a Sales Hero!

BONUSES AND GETTING SUPPORT

Visit **www.FromZeroToSalesHero.com** for these great BONUSES:

1. Sales Activity and Results Tracker
   - The activity tracker accomplishes 3 things: Holds me accountable; drives my daily, weekly, monthly activity; helps me celebrate my wins!
   - Provide instructions as to how you use the tracker: set up weekly, daily, targets: phone calls, appointments, sales, referrals
2. More on The Top 10 Secrets of Top Presenters
   - Rehearse, Rehearse, Rehearse!
   - Have an Intro, Body, Conclusion
   - Intro Sells the Audience on why they should listen
   - Conclusion is a call to action, i.e., here is why this product will benefit you, cost of not changing, etc.
   - Eye Contact is everything
   - The Power of the Pause
   - Keep it Under 20 Minutes; Less PowerPoint, More Flip Charts
   - Speak Up!
   - Screw up? Shut Up!

3. Top Tips: How to Manage Tension and Price Pressure During Negotiations
    - Sales reps give in too often to tension; instead of giving in you can 1-make demands; 2-own your power; 3-if you give a concession, ask for one in return
    - How to Manage Price Pressure: 1-Create elegant negotiables (things that bring the customer value but don't cost you much, i.e., delivery dates, payment terms); 2-Position Value vs. price; 3-Understand the needs vs. the wants
4. Beyond the Sale: How to Grow your Income by Creating Customers for Life
    - Ways to Bring Value to the Customer After the Sale: Quarterly Business Reviews
    - Reference Site
    - Site to trial new products
    - Ask the customer if you can use their testimonial and their name in marketing materials-gives them PR
    - Ask if you can use them for whitepaper/research that the product has met expectations-they benefit from their company recognition in PR
    - Provide refresher training on your product or service to new employees

- o Bring the customer industry insights, latest industry trends or research that can help them or their business succeed and avoid industry pitfalls
5. BONUS CHAPTER
   - o Words speak louder than actions...in the world of sales!
   - o Expect the unexpected
   - o Regaining Control: My favorite buzz phrases and responses
   - o 23 words to avoid in front of a prospect
   - o Less is better

If you have any questions about the processes and concepts in this book, please visit www.AIMwithAmy.com.

AIM Training and Consulting, Inc. provides sales training and coaching for emerging businesses and sales professionals led by a Fortune 50 Top Sales Performer.

AIM: **A**ction + **I**nspiration + **M**otivation = RESULTS!

ACKNOWLEDGEMENTS

As I wrote this book I couldn't help but think of decades of sales mentors, leaders, and everyone that inspired me along this journey of success. Although the sales profession seems like an individual sport, it is far from that — it is a team effort, and it takes a village. I want to thank some that have always been there for me along this journey.

I would like to thank my parents. My late father Bill was a sales representative and then a sales manager early in his career, before he started his own business. He taught me the importance of self-discipline, working smart, selfless determination, competition, self-pride, and what it takes to be an independently wealthy and successful entrepreneur. He taught me the value of education and that you never settle for less than you are capable of delivering. I learned from him 'the pain of discipline is better than the pain of regret.' My mom, Polly, whose sales career path I followed, has taught me so much, and I thank her for being my personal mentor. I remember her pep talks when I wanted to quit! Mom always reminds me that there is a bright side in life and in everything. Sales can be fun, and we don't have to take ourselves so seriously all the time.

117

Her magnetic, charismatic personality is a constant reminder to me that people buy from whom they like. She is selfless and treats everyone with compassion. Her energy and spirit are amazing and inspires me. She always makes me smile.

My husband Andreas is my bedrock. Andreas is my support, my best friend, and the one person who can always help me see that everything is a learning experience. He has always supported me in taking on new life directions without fear. When my world is crazy, he reminds me, with his adventurous spirit, that life is a journey to enjoy and appreciate. He also is my mentor for strength, assertiveness, and not being afraid to take big steps in life. His inner peace and appreciating the tranquility of a sunrise, the sunset, nature, or watching the stars, helps me stay centered.

ABOUT THE AUTHOR

Amy Simatos is an International Corporate Sales Trainer, Coach, Sales Professional, Author, and Distinguished Toastmaster. She has trained hundreds of business entrepreneurs, sales professionals, and clinical teams on sales skills, public speaking, program presentation expertise, sales process, and negotiation skills. She has been recognized as a Fortune 50 Corporate Top Sales Performer, Field Sales Trainer and has been in the sales and marketing profession for over 21 years. She has represented Ameritech, Automatic Data Processing, Datex-Ohmeda, Cardinal Health, and CareFusion corporations.

Amy's true passion is to help other sales professionals be top performers. She attributes her success to her self-discipline, passion, finding resourcefulness during the most complex sales opportunities, and mentoring other sales professionals to succeed to become the sales professionals and presenters they want to be.

She is the CEO of AIM (Action + Inspiration + Motivation = Results) Training and Consulting, Inc. **www.AIMwithAmy.com** where she also provides customized sales coaching and group sales training.

89042600R00075

Made in the USA
Lexington, KY
22 May 2018